Reach Your Potential
CAPRICORN

Teresa Moorey

Dedication

For Howard, my Capricorn rock

Orders: please contact Bookpoint Ltd, 39 Milton Park, Abingdon, Oxon OX14
4TD. Telephone: (44) 01235 400414, Fax: (44) 01235 400454. Lines are open
from 9.00–6.00, Monday to Saturday, with a 24 hour message answering service.
Email address: orders@bookpoint.co.uk

British Library Cataloguing in Publication Data
A catalogue record for this title is available from The British Library

ISBN 0 340 69718 0

First published 1998
Impression number 11   10   9   8   7   6   5   4   3   2
Year   2004   2003   2002   2001   2000   1999   1998

Typeset by Transet Limited, Coventry, England.
Printed in Great Britain for Hodder & Stoughton Educational, a division of
Hodder Headline plc, 338 Euston Road, London NW1 3BH by Cox and Wyman,
Reading, Berks.

Contents

Introduction

A PERSPECTIVE OF ASTROLOGY

Interest in the mystery and significance of the heavens is perhaps as old as humanity. If we can cast our imaginations back, to a time when there were no street lamps, televisions or even books, if we can picture how it must have been to have nothing to do through the deep nights of winter other than to sit and weave stories by the fire at the cave mouth, then we can come close to sensing how important the great dome of stars must have seemed in ancient times.

We are prone to believe that we are wiser today, having progressed beyond old superstitions. We know that all stars are like our Sun – giant nuclear reactors. We know that the planets are lumps of rock reflecting sunlight, they are not gods or demons. But how wise are we in truth? Our growing accumulation of facts brings us no closer to discovering the real meaning behind life. It may well be that our cave-dwelling ancestors knew better than us the meaning of holism. The study of astrology may be part of a journey towards a more holistic perception, taking us, as it does, through the fertile, and often uncharted realms of our own personality.

Until the seventeenth century astrology (which searches for the meaning of heavenly patterns) and astronomy (which seeks to clarify facts about the skies) were one, and it was the search for meanings, not facts that inspired the earliest investigations. Lunar phases have been found carved on bone and stone figures from as early as 15,000BCE (Before Common Era). Astrology then evolved through the civilisations of Mesopotamia, Greece and others.

Through the 'dark ages' much astrological lore was preserved in Islamic countries, but in the fifteenth century astrology grew in popularity in the West. Queen Elizabeth I had her own personal astrologer, John Dee, and such fathers of modern astronomy as Kepler and Galileo served as court astrologers in Europe.

Astrology was taught at the University of Salamanca until 1776. What is rarely appreciated is that some of our greatest scientists, notably Newton and even Einstein, were led to their discoveries by intuition. Newton was a true mystic, and it was the search for meaning – the same motivation that inspired the Palaeolithic observer – that gave rise to some of our most brilliant advances. Indeed Newton is widely believed to have been an astrologer. The astronomer Halley, who discovered the famous comet, is reported to have criticised Newton for this, whereupon Sir Isaac replied 'I have studied it Sir, you have not!'

During the twentieth century astrology enjoyed a revival, and in 1948 The Faculty of Astrological Studies was founded, offering tuition of high quality and an examination system. The great psychologist Carl Jung was a supporter of astrology, and his work has expanded ideas about the mythic connections of the birth chart. Astrology is still eyed askance by many people, and there is no doubt that there is little purely scientific corroboration for astrology – the exception to this is the exhaustive statistical work undertaken by the Gauquelins. Michel Gauquelin was a French statistician whose research shows undeniable connection between professional prominence and the position of planets at birth. Now that the concept of a mechanical universe is being superseded, there is a greater chance that astrology and astronomy will reunite.

Anyone who consults a good astrologer comes away deeply impressed by the insight of the birth chart. Often it is possible to see very deeply into the personality and to be able to throw light on current dilemmas. It is noteworthy that even the most sceptical of people tend to know their Sun sign and the characteristics associated with it.

■ WHAT IS A BIRTH CHART?

Your birth chart is a map of the heavens drawn up for the time, date and place of your birth. An astrologer will prefer you to be as accurate as you can about the time of day, for that affects the sign rising on the eastern horizon. This 'rising sign' is very important to your personality. However, if you do not know your birth time a chart can still be compiled for you. There will be some details missing, but useful interpretations may still be made. It is far better for the astrologer to know that your birth time is in question than to operate from a position of false certainty. The birth chart for Elvis Presley (page 4) is a simplified chart. Additional factors would be entered on the chart and considered by an astrologer, such as angles (aspects) between the planets, and the houses.

The birth chart shows each of the planets and the Moon in the astrological signs, and can be thought of as an 'energy map' of the different forces operating within the psyche. Thus the Sun sign (often called 'birth sign' or 'star sign') refers only to the position of the Sun. If the planets are in very different signs from the Sun sign, the interpretation will be greatly modified. Thus, if a person has Sun in Leo yet is somewhat introverted or quiet, this may be because the Moon was in reserved Capricorn when that person was born. Nonetheless, the Sun represents the light of consciousness, the integrating force, and most people recognise that they are typical of their Sun sign, although in some people it will be more

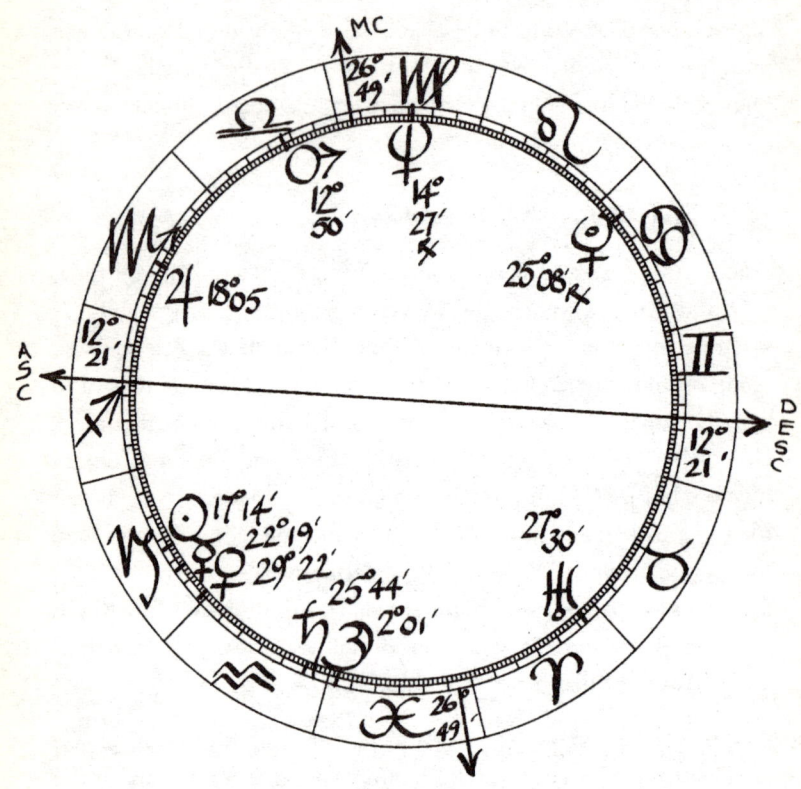

The birth chart of Elvis Presley
Known as 'The Pelvis', the singer exemplified the 'Saturnalian' aspect of
Capricorn, but also to a lesser extent the conventional, for he was shown
accepting army draft and succeeded in becoming an institution.

noticeable than in others. The planets Mercury and Venus are very
close to the Sun and often occupy the same sign, so intensifying the
Sun-sign influence.

The **planets** are life principles, energy centres. To enable you to understand the birth chart, here are their glyphs:

Sun	☉	Jupiter	♃
Moon	☽	Saturn	♄
Mercury	☿	Uranus	♅
Venus	♀	Neptune	♆
Mars	♂	Pluto	♇ (♇)

Rising Sign or **Ascendant** (**ASC**) is the way we have of meeting the world, our outward persona. **Midheaven** (**MC**) refers to our image, aspirations, how we like to be seen.

The **signs** are modes of expression, ways of being. Here are their glyphs:

Aries	♈	Libra	♎
Taurus	♉	Scorpio	♏
Gemini	♊	Sagittarius	♐
Cancer	♋	Capricorn	♑
Leo	♌	Aquarius	♒
Virgo	♍	Pisces	♓

Using knowledge of the glyphs you can see that the Sun is in

This book is written about your Sun sign, because the Sun sign serves as an accessible starting point for those wishing to learn about themselves through astrology. However, do not let your interest stop there. If you find anything helpful in comments and advice stemming from Sun sign alone, you will find your true birth chart even more revealing. The address of the Faculty of Astrological Studies appears in 'Further Reading and Resources' at the back of this book, and it is a good idea to approach them for a list of trained astrologers who can help you. Moon *phase* at birth (as distinct from Moon sign) is also very important. *The Moon and You for Beginners* (see 'Further Reading') explains this fascinating area clearly, and provides a simple chart for you to look up your Moon phase, and learn what this means for your personality.

■ HOW DOES ASTROLOGY WORK?

We cannot explain astrology by the usual methods of cause and effect. In fact, there are many things we cannot explain. No one can define exactly what life is. We do not know exactly what electricity is, but we know how to use it. Few of us have any idea how a television set works, but we know how to turn it on. Although we are not able to explain astrology we are still able to use it, as any capable astrologer will demonstrate.

Jung discovered something called 'synchronicity'. This he defined as 'an acausal connecting principle'. Simply, this means that some events have a meaningful connection *other than cause and effect*. The planets do not cause us to do things, but their movements are synchronistic with our lives. The old dictum 'as above, so below' applies here. It is a mystery. We can't explain it, but that doesn't mean we should refuse to believe in it. A little boy on a visit to the circus saw an elephant for the first time and said 'There's no such thing'. We may laugh at the little boy, but how many of us respond to things we do not understand in this way?

The planetary positions in your birth chart are synchronistic with the time of your birth, when you took on separate existence, and they are synchronistic with your individuality in this life. They have much to say about you.

■ MYTH AND PSYCHOLOGY

The planets are named after the old gods and goddesses of Rome, which in turn link in with Greek and other pantheons. The planets represent 'life principles' – forces that drive the personality, and as such they can be termed 'archetypal'. This means that they are basic ideas, universal within human society and are also relevant in terms of the forces that, in some inexplicable way, inhabit the corners of the universe and inform the Earth and all human institutions. Thus the assertive energy that is represented by Mars means energetic action of all sorts – explosions and fires, wars, fierce debates and personal anger. Put briefly, here are the meanings of the planets:

- Mercury – intellect and communication
- Venus – love, unifying, relating
- Mars – assertion, energy, fighting spirit
- Jupiter – expansion, confidence, optimism
- Saturn – limitation, discipline
- Uranus – rebellion, independence
- Neptune – power to seek the ideal, sense the unseen
- Pluto – power to transform and evolve

These principles are modified according to the astrological sign they inhabit; thus Venus in Pisces may be gently loving, dreamy and self-sacrificing, while Venus in Aries will be demanding and adventurous in relationships. Thus the planets in signs form a complex psychological framework – and that is only part of the story of chart interpretation!

In the old mythologies these 'energies' or 'archetypes' or 'gods' were involved in classical dramas. An example is the story of Saturn and Uranus. Uranus is the rejecting father of Saturn, who later castrates and murders his father – thus innovative people reject reactionaries, who then murder them, so the revolutionary part of the personality is continually 'killed off' by the restrictive part. The exact positions and angles between the planets will indicate how this and other myths may come to life. In addition, the mere placement of planets by sign – and, of course, especially the Sun sign, call forth various myths as illustrations. The ancient myths are good yarns but they are inspired and vivid dramatisations of what may be going on repeatedly within your personality and that of your nearest and dearest. Myths are used by many modern psychologists and therapists in a tradition that has grown since Jung. We shall be using mythic themes to illustrate internal dynamics in this book.

■ THE SIGNS OF THE ZODIAC

There are twelve signs, and each of these belongs to an Element – Earth, Fire, Air or Water, and a Quality – Cardinal, Fixed or Mutable. The Cardinal signs are more geared to action, the Fixed

SIGN	QUALITY	ELEMENT
Aries	Cardinal	Fire
Taurus	Fixed	Earth
Gemini	Mutable	Air
Cancer	Cardinal	Water
Leo	Fixed	Fire
Virgo	Mutable	Earth
Libra	Cardinal	Air
Scorpio	Fixed	Water
Sagittarius	Mutable	Fire
Capricorn	Cardinal	Earth
Aquarius	Fixed	Air
Pisces	Mutable	Water

tend to remain stable and rooted, whereas the Mutable signs are adaptable, changeable.

Jung defined four functions of consciousness – four different ways of perceiving the world – 'thinking', 'feeling', 'sensation' and 'intuition'. Thinking is the logical, evaluative approach that works in terms of the mind. Feeling is also evaluative, but this time in relation to culture and family needs. This is not the same as emotion, although 'feeling' people often process emotions more smoothly than other types. Jung saw 'feeling' as rational, too. 'Sensation' refers to the 'here and now', the five physical senses, while 'intuition' relates to lives in terms of the possible, to visions and hunches. Jung taught that we tend to have one function uppermost in consciousness, another one or maybe two secondary and another repressed or 'inferior', although we all possess each of these functions to some degree.

Jungian ideas are being refined and expanded, and they are incorporated into modern methods of personality testing, as in the Myers-Briggs test. If a prospective employer has recently given you such a test, it was to establish your talents and potential for the job. However, the basic four-fold division is still extremely useful, and I find that it is often of great help in assisting clients to understand themselves, and their partners, in greater depth – for we are all apt to assume that everyone processes information and applies it in the same way as we do. But they don't! It is worthy of mention that the important categories of 'introverted' and 'extraverted' were also identified by Jung. In astrology, Fire and Air signs seem to be extraverted, generally speaking, and Earth and Water introverted – and this has been borne out by the statistical research of the astrologer, Jeff Mayo. However, this doesn't mean that all feeling and sensation people are introverted and all intuitives and thinkers extraverted – this is definitely not the case, and calls for more detailed examination of the chart (e.g. lots of Fire and Water may mean an extravert feeling type).

Very broadly speaking we may link the Fire signs to intuition, Water to feeling, Earth to sensation and Air to thinking. Often thinking and feeling are drawn together and sensation and intuition are attracted, because they are opposites. This probably happens because we all seek to become more whole, but the process can be painful. The notion of the four functions, when understood, does help to throw light on some of the stumbling blocks we often encounter in relationships. However, some people just do not seem to fit. Also Fire doesn't always correspond to intuition, Water to feeling, etc. – it seems this is usually the case, but not all astrologers agree. Some link Fire with feeling, Water with intuition, and most agree that other chart factors are also important. As with all theories, this can be used to help, expand and clarify, not as a rigid system to impose definitions. We shall be learning more about these matters in relation to the Sun sign in the following pages.

■ THE PRECESSION OF THE EQUINOXES

One criticism often levelled at astrology is that 'the stars have moved' and so the old signs are invalid. There is some truth in this, and it is due to a phenomenon called 'The Precession of the Equinoxes'. The beginning of the sign Aries occurs when the Sun is overhead at the equator, moving northwards. This is called the Spring Equinox, for now day and night are equal all over the globe, and the first point of Aries is called the 'equinoctial point'. Because the Earth not only turns on its axis but 'rocks' on it (imagine a giant knitting needle driven through the poles – the Earth spins on this, but the head of the needle also slowly describes a circle in space) the 'equinoctial point' has moved against the background of stars. Thus, when the Sun is overhead at the equator, entering Aries, it is no longer at the start of the constellation of Aries, where it occurred when the signs were named, but is now in the constellation of Pisces. The 'equinoctial point' is moving backwards into Aquarius, hence the ideas of the dawning 'Aquarian age'.

So where does that leave astrology? Exactly in the same place, in actuality. For it all depends on how you think the constellations came to be named in the first place. Did our ancestors simply look up and see the shape of a Ram in the sky? Or did they – being much more intuitive and in tune with their surroundings than we are – feel sharply aware of the quality, the energies around at a certain time of the year, and *then* look skyward, translating what they sensed into a suitable starry symbol? This seems much more likely – and you have only to look at the star groups to see that it takes a fair bit of imagination to equate most of them with the figures they represent! The Precession of the Equinoxes does not affect astrological interpretation, for it is based upon observation and intuition, rather than 'animals in the sky'.

■ USING THIS BOOK

Reach Your Potential – Capricorn explores your Sun sign and what this means in terms of your personality; the emphasis is on self-exploration. All the way through, hints are given to help you to begin to understand yourself better, ask questions about yourself and use what you have to maximum effect. This book will show you how to use positive Capricornian traits to your best advantage, and how to neutralise negative Capricornian traits. Don't forget that by reading it you are consenting, however obliquely, to the notion that you are connected in strange and mysterious ways to the web of the cosmos. What happens within you is part of a meaningful pattern that you can explore and become conscious of, thereby acquiring greater influence on the course of your life. Let this encourage you to ask further questions.

Some famous Capricorns

Janis Joplin, David Bowie, Eddy Shah, Sarah Miles, Paul Cézanne, Humphrey Bogart, Pablo Casals, Nat King Cole, Benjamin Franklin, Ava Gardner, Cary Grant, J. Edgar Hoover, Joan of Arc, Johannes Kepler, Martin Luther King, Rudyard Kipling, Mao Tse Tung, Henry Miller, Isaac Newton, Richard Nixon, Louis Pasteur, Edgar Allen Poe, Helena Rubenstein, Loretta Young, J. R. Tolkien, Muhammed Ali, Joan Baez, Elvis Presley, Annie Lennox, Simone de Beauvoir, Gurdieff, Carlos Castaneda, Marlene Dietrich, Ingrid Bergman, Elizabeth Arden.

Naturally, anyone in public life will find the tenacity, ambition and practicality of a strong Capricorn very much an asset.

Climbing, tethered or stuck-in-the-mud – what sort of Capricorn are you?

Here is a quiz to give you an idea of how you are operating at the moment. Its tone is light hearted, but the intent is serious and you may learn something interesting about yourself. Don't think too hard about the answers, just pick the one that appeals to you most.

1. **You have been asked to arrange the office party. How do you react?**

    a) ☐ Is this someone's idea of a joke? You rarely go to parties if you can help it. You decide you will go out and buy a 'How To Throw a Party' manual.

    b) ☐ You'll do it the same as it was done last year, only even more efficiently. You begin to make notes and lists.

    c) ☐ They obviously asked you because they know you're pretty good at this sort of thing. You'll make sure nothing runs out, and that the Chair is well looked after (and you'll arrange a Gorilla-gram for later).

2. **You have gone home with that special person who now seems hell-bent on having sex with you on the kitchen table. So you:**

    a) ☐ Feel instantly turned off. It's all too out of control and unpredictable – and someone might come in.

    b) ☐ Edge your way towards the sitting room, hoping he or she doesn't have a fetish about pine.

    c) ☐ Lock the back door – and wey-hey!

3. **You have an important job interview coming up. How do you prepare?**

    a) ☐ You get your clothes cleaned and shoes polished – but you know you won't get it. You should be so lucky! You prepare yourself in advance for rejection and tell yourself you won't be upset.

b) ☐ You look deeply into the solvency of the company and its record of industrial unrest. You are rather worried about making a move.

c) ☐ You learn as much as possible about how the company works, your prospective boss and the post for which you have applied.

4. **How do you feel about holidays? Do you look forward to them, plan them, etc?**

a) ☐ You don't go on holiday if you can help it.

b) ☐ You go on holiday as long as you can take your mobile phone, laptop and Filofax. You aren't too bothered where, but once you have decided you make the arrangements, or at least oversee them.

c) ☐ You'll go almost anywhere but you like to keep occupied and to have control of most of the arrangements.

5. **Someone pays you a compliment. How do you react?**

a) ☐ You wonder what she or he might want from you, to butter you up like that.

b) ☐ You feel embarrassed and act gruff to cover it.

c) ☐ You feel warm inside that what you are or have done has been appreciated.

6. **What do you do in your spare time?**

a) ☐ Spare time – what's that?

b) ☐ You work out your finances.

c) ☐ You do something creative or productive – you like to see a result.

7. **A family member or flatmate has apparently moved something essential to your life, for example your watch. What do you do?**

a) ☐ You *always* put your watch on the shelf, on the landing, before you go to bed, and put it on in the morning when you come out of the bathroom. You are outraged and put out for the entire day.

b) ☐ Although you are annoyed, you are gratified that your providence has proved justified, in that you have a spare one tucked away. You rummage to find it and end up cross because you are late.

c) ☐ It's not worth disrupting your schedule for that. You'll find out what happened later, and maybe pick up a cheap one at the garage to tide you over.

8. **As Chair of a committee, at work or socially, you find your ruling is challenged by two members. How do you react?**

a) ☐ You are the Chair and they should not put you on the spot like that. You become cold and autocratic.

b) ☐ You give way, reluctantly, inch by inch.

c) ☐ You invite comments and efficiently chair a debate on the matter.

9. **Your car breaks down on the way to an important engagement. Now what do you do?**

a) ☐ This always happens to you and it just goes to show that life is always against you. You get home as best you can and kick yourself for being too thrifty to have it serviced.

b) ☐ You gloomily assume repairs will cost a bomb and ponder the cost of a taxi. Then you lift the bonnet and have a look yourself.

c) ☐ This is life, and you have funds stashed against car wear-and-tear. You call a taxi, irritated that you will be late.

Now count up your score. What do you have most of – a's, b's or c's?

Mostly a's. You really are somewhat stuck-in-the-mud at the moment, aren't you? Is it realistic to be quite so gloomy? Aren't you simply making things worse for yourself? Where is all that self-reliance, practicality and common sense? You are the architect of your life and the captain of your soul. Haul yourself up by your bootstraps and get a life.

Mostly b's. Mostly you are a capable person, and because you cope quite well (albeit a little gloomily) you may not have noticed that you are going round in circles on your tether. Stand back a bit and get a wider perspective on your life. Take off your blinkers – you are probably erecting your own barriers. Where do you want to get to, or what do you want to achieve? Isn't is time you set your sights on a goal and started to climb?

Mostly c's. You're a climbing Goat, with the propensity to become a high-flyer. It takes a lot to faze you, and your ability to cope is often awesome – what is more, you haven't lost the ability to enjoy yourself, which is one of your creative secrets. Don't intimidate people or be tempted to use them. And remember, even *you* can't be prepared for everything, so cultivate an inner strength to help you through the unforeseen.

If you found that in many cases none of the answers came anywhere near to fitting you, then it may be that you are an uncharacteristic Capricorn. This may be because there are factors in your astrological chart that frustrate the expression of your Sun sign, or it may be that there is a preponderance of other signs, outweighing the Capricorn part. Whatever the case may be, your Sun-sign potential needs to be realised. Perhaps you will find something to help ring a few bells in the following pages.

1 The essential Capricorn

What is conservatism? Is it not adherence to the old and tried, against the new and untried?

Abraham Lincoln

I love everything that's old: old friends, old times, old manners, old books, old wine

Oliver Goldsmith, *She Stoops To Conquer*

■ PLODDERS AND POWER-SEEKERS

Capricorn, the dutiful and provident, is not especially known for playing roles. And yet there is much more to the average Capricorn than meets the eye. There are greater matters passing beneath that guarded exterior than the grand plan of proceeding from birth to death in a respectable fashion. Yet the only thing that Capricorn is likely to wear on a crisply tailored sleeve is a subtle and tasteful status symbol – such as an onyx cufflink or expensive bracelet. The heart – be it of granite or gold – is rarely glimpsed. From Billy-goat Gruff to Giddy Goat, what you get, if you wait patiently, is often much more than you see.

Tenacity, practicality, caution – these are laudable Capricornian qualities. However, they have all the allure of the average Victorian school-marm. It is true that Capricorn may lack a superficial glamour, but this, more than any other sign, is that of the achiever. Capricorn may drudge and trudge, take a back seat and even turn the other cheek, but underneath the Goat is following a hidden agenda that can be summed up as – power. It may not be obvious for many years, even to the Goat, quite what the objective might be.

But time that waits for no man is often a friend to Capricorn. Not all, but most Capricorns do in the end achieve positions of mastery, dominance, or at the least effectuality. This is a sign tailored to make a difference in the world. What price all the razzamatazz, when, as everyone knows, power is the greatest turn-on of all?

■ CAPRICORN BODY LANGUAGE

Much about this sign can be encapsulated as 'economical'. Movements are no exception. You don't waste energy on flamboyant mannerisms. In any case, sweeping gestures might be a threat to the heirlooms. A strong Capricorn inclines to folded arms, closed mouth and closed fists. The air is usually dignified, and many Capricorns appear older than their years, when young, while becoming increasingly youthful as the years pass. You are usually aware of your body space – you do not welcome encroachment and may shrink from involuntary touch. Rarely do you sprawl or invade the space of others. Your movements are sometimes a little diffident, but your walk is often very decisive, feet making crisp contact with the ground. You are rarely obtrusive, believing that there is no advantage in drawing attention to oneself for the sake of it, but when you do decide to speak up you have the knack of being heard. Occasionally there may be evidence of tense habits, such as nail-biting or lip-chewing, but these rarely have the effect of making the Goat look raggedy. Posture is often excellent and the general effect is one of meticulous but understated care.

■ MYTHS OF THE GOAT

When we consider this symbolic animal the tailored and conventional Capricornian image seems to disappear at a glance, and we are brought up closer to the essential nature of the sign. What do we know about goats? They are climbers, yes. They eat just about anything, including the lace off one's underwear, if they can get it. They are earthy, horny animals (in fact a lady who bred goats told me that no smell is so strong or so ineradicable as that of the billy goat). They give copious milk and have associations with the rustic charm of Arcadia; creatures of the Earth Mother, indeed. With the loss of the wild places of the Earth and the subjugation of nature, part of the essential Capricorn has been lost.

Rhea, Amalthea and Blodeuwedd

Rhea, the great mountain mother, gave birth to the Olympian gods of Greece, notably their king, Zeus. She has links with the goat, and it was to the magical goat-goddess Amalthea that she fostered out her son Zeus, so that he might be safe from the jealousy of his father, Saturn/Chronos (more of Chronos later). As he grew to strength, Zeus broke off one of the goat's horns, which turned into the wonderful 'cornucopia' – the horn of plenty and gift of the Goddess that nourishes all of humankind. Then the goat was transformed into the starry constellation of Capricorn.

Another story tells of Amalthea's mating with the rampant goat-foot god, Pan, from which union was born the goat-fish, Aigokeres. Aigokeres is the Greek word for Capricorn, and Capricorn is often depicted as a goat with the tail of a fish. One myth tells how Pan became a goat-fish, like the Babylonian Ea, who came from the sea and instructed humans in all the arts of civilisation. This speaks of Capricorn's instinctual links with the mysteries of the primal waters, and hints at a more arcane aspect to this sign. Other European stories tell of the love-goddess appearing to her beloved clad in a net and riding upon a goat. Goats are also associated with the Welsh Goddess, Blodeuwedd. This goddess was fashioned from oak, broom and meadowsweet by a magician, although her face was as lovely as a flower, the black heart of nature beat within her and motivated by unbridled lust she plotted with her lover to slay her husband, Llew. Far from being a cheap adulteress, Blodeuwedd embodies the inexorability of natural law, and Llew is a representation of the Sun god who must die each year in order to be reborn.

So, with these myths in mind, we find within our Capricornian pillar of society something that answers to no law but that of the wilderness. Something that is very uncivilised indeed.

■ ELEMENT, QUALITY AND RULING PLANET

We have seen that each of the signs of the zodiac belongs to one of the Elements, Earth, Fire, Air or Water, and one of the Qualities, Cardinal, Fixed or Mutable. Capricorn is Cardinal Earth. Earthy people concentrate primarily on the evidence of their senses. They are rarely given to far-flung speculation, to dreams, schemes and intangibles. Capricorn is certainly no exception to this, realising that what endures is built upon solid ground. However, Capricorn in its 'cardinal' aspect is creative and constructive. These are climbers, and when you climb with determination you eventually reach the top. There, feet planted upon hard rock, there is nothing to aim for but the stars. So the cardinal nature of Capricorn sometimes leads them at length to attempt more than material achievement, although they will always seek to ground their theories, testing everything in practical terms and wanting to see physical effect and change.

We have seen that the Element Earth has some things in common with what Jung called the 'sensation' function. This doesn't mean, of course, that Earthy people are 'sensationalists', for this is not the case at all. It simply means that these people put their trust in the concrete. More subtle types may find this approach lacking or incomprehensible, but it is wonderfully concentrating and secure. Capricorn is strongly identified with what she or he touches, makes and inhabits. However in this, the last of the Earth signs, we do occasionally glimpse traces of the magician. This may be no more than the skilful mastery of one practised at handling the world, and certainly many Capricorns are scornful about anything smacking of the mysterious, as they may be about 'silly' ideas like altruism, idealism, mysticism. However, I have observed in not a few Capricorns a yearning after something more and a knowledge that all their achievements amount to very little unless they can be a stepping-stone to something of wider significance. Aware of the limitations imposed by time, Capricorn may become alive to the limits of a temporal approach, and seek something that could be called eternal – in a sensible fashion, of course!

Capricorn is the tenth sign of the zodiac and the final sign of the Earth trilogy. The Fire of Aries, first and Pioneering sign, was followed by Earthy Taurus the Farmer and then by Airy Gemini, the Communicator and Traveller. With Cancer, first Water sign, we discovered the importance of Family bonds and with Leo the signature of the Monarch. Virgo, second Earth sign of the Sower and Reaper was followed by Airy, diplomatic Libra, sign of Human Relationships, and then by passionate Watery Scorpio, deepening us to the secrets of the human heart. Last of the Fire signs, Sagittarius the Philosopher brings us up to date with Capricorn, the Builder. And so we see the pattern of human society taking shape. As we progress, the signs tend to become more complex, and there is little doubt that Capricorn is the most complicated of the Earthy triad.

In the Northern Hemisphere the Sun enters Capricorn at the darkest, coldest time of the year, and for a few days the Sun seems to stand still (the meaning of 'solstice') before gaining momentum. This marks the ancient festival of Yule, and in many mythologies it coincides with the time when the Sun-god is born of the Mother Goddess. From the depths of the dark and barren earth the spark of new life is born. We welcome this with Christmas festivities, giving presents to each other as we would to any new baby – to the Sun-god. And so Capricorn is the season both of darkness, the ground hard and hoary with frost, and the time of fertility and celebration. We are at the heart of nature's mystery.

For those of you who live in the Southern Hemisphere, the Sun is just passing the Midsummer solstice, beginning the descent again to winter. Vegetation may be at the height of its splendour and yet the darkness comes. These are Capricorn themes, both of ending and fertility, the rewards of time and its destructive march as life returns to the secret places within the earth. The Southern Hemisphere is a mirror image of the meanings apparent in the Northern.

Each sign is said to have a 'Ruling Planet'. This means that there is a planet that has a special affinity with the sign, whose energies are most at home when expressed in terms of that sign. The Ruling Planet for Capricorn is Saturn. Saturn, in ancient times, was believed to be the outermost planet, deep in the blackness of space and forming a limit, or 'skin' to the solar system. The symbolism of perimeter, outer limit, is reinforced by Saturn's rings (we now know rings are also present around Uranus and Neptune). The god Saturn, and his Greek counterpart Cronos, is a dour deity, bringing endings and death, clinging meanly, rapaciously – and even murderously – to power, and showing us just where 'the shoe pinches'. He is also shown as 'Old Father Time' and the Grim Reaper. However, the sickle he holds is an oblique salute to the Mother Goddess, in her guise as crescent Moon. Saturn is also linked with a Golden Age, with the cornucopia and with the just rewards of labours. Here we have a repetition of the themes of restriction, duty, authority linked to more instinctual, primal forces, as personified by the Moon, and seen also to have an abundant and fertile aspect.

■ BOY SCOUTS AND GIRL GUIDES

'Be prepared' is the motto of the true Capricorn. The Goat can spend so much time saving for the 'rainy day' that the sunshine passes unnoticed. But Capricorn is not just financially prepared. I know one Capricorn who goes around like Inspector Gadget, a tool for every conceivable job concealed about his person, including a corkscrew (he never drinks wine away from home because he always does the driving) and a pick to extract stones from horses' hooves (he has never ridden a horse in his life). In addition, his mobile phone is attached to his belt whenever he goes as far as the garden gate, and he possesses no fewer than six Filofaxes, which no doubt weigh on his mind but never seem to bow his straight, Capricorn shoulders. Of course, if you are overprepared you simply meet yourself coming backwards, or find that lesser mortals have sabotaged your plans. I knew a Capricorn who always liked to lay the table for his breakfast the night before, and abandoned this only when sharing lodgings with a jolly Irishman who came home hungry late at night and munched gratefully on the cornflakes that some kind soul had apparently provided. I am sure that my Capricorn husband takes so long to get out of the house in the morning simply because all the paraphernalia he has assembled in advance the previous evening gets in his way!

Capricorns, in common with the other Earth signs, do not trust the future – hence the need for preparation. In fact, it has to be said that Capricorn feels safe only if there is something to worry about.

'Hope for the best, prepare for the worst' could be another Capricornian refrain. Capricorn has been called pessimistic, but that is not quite accurate. Only the most embittered Goat believes that the worst always happens. What most Capricorns do believe, however, is that the worst surely *will* happen if you have not done all in your power to prevent it. Eternally circumspect, practical and cautious, the Goat accepts that the world is a conspiracy to catch him or her out, and usually succeeds in averting this. But there is a cost. Someone once said that 'The trouble with keeping both feet on the ground is that you can never get your pants off!' Many Capricorns never discover the Saturnalian delights that are their birthright because they are so concerned with watching their backs! These Goats need to remember that limits are things they deal well in – and there are limits to how well prepared they can be. Endless preparation can create the very thing it is designed to avert – a life of worry and misery. So, accept there are limits to how prepared even you can be and know when the time has come to let your hair – and may be other things – down.

◼ GIDDY GOATS

From ancient times the Winter Solstice has been celebrated, and the Romans dedicated it to their Lord of Time, Saturn. Far from being sombre, this was a crazy season of indulgence, pranks and role reversal, when slaves became masters and masters slaves. Here we glimpse the orgiastic aspect of Capricorn that is generally obscured behind the business suit or overalls – or just behind the dutiful mask. Yes, there is a wild side to Capricorn that dances to the pipes of Pan but follows no polite code. A something that is primitive and unutterably ancient, that obeys the laws of the quest-ing root, the rutting beast, the rhythm of the rainfall, but knows nothing of civilisation. This is so far from our picture of stalwart Capricorn that we may find it unrecognisable. However, peep out it does, Goblin-like, when Capricorn displays that dry wit or drops the wallflower image and starts dancing on the tables. It is there in Capricornian sexuality, too, when the work schedule has been laid aside to permit it. Indeed, in some Capricorns the 'wild' side may be the most obvious – as in some Capricorn celebrities, such as David Bowie and Rod Stewart.

How may we understand this aspect, which seems to make the sign appear almost schizophrenic? Quite simply, in fact, when we think in terms of the Earth. Earth has her charter and it decrees a season for all. There is a time, to till the soil, with the sweat of your brow, to sow seeds, to reap and store, to build and toil. There is also a season to ramble in the Greenwood, to breathe of the heady blossom and to mate and enjoy. There are no appeals against the edicts of Earth – her rule is absolute. She demands complete identification with purpose, and Capricorn as her dutiful child, usually obeys. However, many Capricorns follow the letter of the law, rather than the spirit, and some follow laws for laws' sake, forgetting Earth's most important commandment – to dance, sing, feast, make music and love all in praise of the Earth, for her law is love unto all beings. Our cultural alienation from nature has not been kind to Capricorn. Estranged from the primal law, which is not there to limit or punish but to provide a concrete framework, Capricorn often becomes hedged about with 'shoulds' and 'oughts' that frustrate every move. Well, you know what any good Goat does with a hedge! Chew through it and head for the hills!

■ THE END JUSTIFIES THE MEANS

We are apt to suspect anyone who is generally dutiful and conventional of a certain amount of hypocrisy. We wonder what lies below the surface – and rightly so! No one can be that good, surely? The answer is no, not in the case of Capricorn, and a cross section of the straight-and-true Capricorn may reveal a knot of manipulation and double dealing. Not that this means that Capricorn is not to be trusted, for many would die rather than be guilty of deceit. However, most Capricorns have a grain of cynicism and self-centred calculation. They cannot be faulted for that, for it is a survival mechanism, and a very sensible one, and as long as it doesn't masquerade as altruism we can respect it. But there are some Capricorns who take this much too far. Perhaps the most notable of these was the Capricornian US president, Richard Nixon, whose famous Watergate machinations have given us the suffix '-gate' for any dubious public affair.

What lies behind this, and how can you find such actions acceptable? Part of the answer lies simply in Capricornian pragmatism – the end justifies the means, get results, achieve the objective. There are certain situations where that is fine, and such an attitude contributes to the effectuality of many of you Capricorns. Get where you need to get to by the best route, even if that means deviating from the straight and narrow. Most things carry within them the seed of their opposite, as the Chinese yin/yang symbol indicates, and so reliable Capricorn, in the cause of doing what must be done, may become curiously unreliable when it comes to principles. We might be thankful when dry old Capricorn drops the principles for a while, but when this involves the cold and calculating use of other people, this is less forgivable. What is even more unforgivable is the hypocrisy that often conceals it. The 'honest broker' salts away millions while stoutly condemning the greed and deceit of others. Worst of all, such a one often truly believes there is one law for him and another for the rest of us – because what he is doing is for a 'purpose'.

Of course, the average Goat works hard for the daily bread, sleeps the sleep of the just and dreams of one day being company director.

However, some Capricornian standards are not so much ideals as an adherence to 'system' that Goats may not find meaningful, deep down – and then it may be easier to subvert! But members of this sign can feel guilty and burdened by what they have done. All the more reason to formulate your own standards that are worth sticking to. Capricorn is not an overt sign. Your ambitions and ways of achieving them are often known only to yourselves. However, you need to remember that you will never feel the joy of any achievement while you know, in your heart of hearts, it has been gained by questionable means. To the majority of Capricorns a measure of power is likely to be achievable at some point in life. You need to learn faith in your own abilities and in your own future, for no one knows better how to reach your goals. The rewards that are to come should not be tarnished in the process.

■ MASTERY AND MYSTERY

Capricorn wants to achieve the physical, and many Capricorns are builders of one sort or another. However, some Capricorns are not content with this. They wish to extend their proficiency into abstract spheres, or at least see wider implications in what they have done. This can mean a concern for the social order. It can also mean achievements in music, sculpture or other arts or a career in design or engineering. In addition, it can also amount to forays into what can only be called the magical.

How may we understand this better? In the end many Capricorns become aware that all possessions, all acts of construction have no meaning unless an ultimate purpose is expansion of the human spirit. Of course, this may be taken simply for Capricorn power hunger extending even into the realms of the unseen. Truly it is a perception of the spiritual essence within the material world, that is gained not by transcendence but by understanding and identification. This may manifest as an interest in 'Earth mysteries', for example. It can be said that all the Earth signs, in their heart of hearts, hunger for something beyond their five senses, that they do not really believe in, in the light of day, but which may fascinate, or generate unease or sometimes ossify into ritual observances as if to propitiate a spiritual debt collector. From my observation, of all the Earth signs, Capricorn is the most generally open to explore the mysterious realms, and because you do this from the position of the sceptic and the pragmatist, you are able to attain a measure of effectuality that may be denied those who readily drift off into the ether.

The story of Cronos and Ouranus

Cronos/Saturn was one of the children of Gaia, the Earth Goddess and the Sky God, Ouranus. Ouranus, however, was displeased with his monstrous and diverse offspring and insisted upon pushing them back into the womb of their mother, where they could never see the light of day or offend his eye. Naturally, this practice was very uncomfortable for Gaia, and her outrage grew. She enlisted the help of her son, Cronos, and plotted with him a terrible revenge. Furnished with a sharp sickle, Cronos lay in wait in a cave on a mountain top, and when night fell and his father came to lie with his wife, Gaia, Cronos crept out and cut off Ouranus's genitals with a sweep of his gleaming weapon.

Now it was time for Cronos to fulfil the rest of the bargain and to free his brothers and sisters, but he did not oblige. Savage and resentful at the neglect he had endured, he seized power for himself and proceeded to eat his own children in case they should treat him in the way he had his father. But Gaia was not to be cheated. She put a curse upon her son and decreed that he should in turn, be deposed by his own offspring.

His wife Rhea concealed the infant Zeus and gave him a stone to eat instead. Zeus was brought up in seclusion and lived to fulfil the decree of Gaia, taking his place in turn as the king of the Olympian gods. Cronos was then condemned to live in the Underworld.

In this story we see that Cronos/Saturn is in the service of the Earth Mother, in truth. His downfall comes because he betrays her and wishes to claim power for himself. It is best if Capricorn remains faithful to that identification with the Earth, rather than insisting on empty systems and authority that can deprive you of true sovereignty in your own life and consign you to an 'underworld' of depression. It is not an adherence to codes – even if they have been made by Capricorn – that can satisfy, but an identification with the cycles of life and the joy that comes from simply being. Cronos, of course, has given us such words as 'chronology'. Old Father Time he may be, and if Capricorn wishes to be master of time instead of its slave there may be a necessity to stand back, gain a wider perspective and sort out which routines are productive and which are not.

Cronos's Roman counterpart was, of course, Saturn, and it is probable that this name is connected to 'satan'. The Celtic Cernunnos was a god of nature that seems to have links with Cronos (the names are not dissimilar) and he was one of the personifications of the Horned God – like Pan – who were subverted in later years as the devil, but whose horns represented animal vitality. Cernunnos also embodied the culling aspect of nature, for although he was surrounded by a multitude of creatures, he also decided which should die, and when. Here we have Capricornian themes of lust and abundance, coupled with a recognition of structure and necessity. It is a wise Goat who keeps these in balance!

■ PRACTICE AND CHANGE ■

● It is good practice to weigh alternatives and be cautious and circumspect, but don't let this degenerate into general suspicion that prevents you taking up opportunities.

● There is a time for everything, so there is a time for play. Learn to welcome Pan into your life, and live a little.

● Too much pessimism will give you something to be pessimistic about. Think carefully about your life strategy. It may keep you safe from some difficulties, but is it also confining and depressing you? Take positive action.

● Make sure your own preparations do not, in fact, get in your way. For instance, endless lists of jobs may be so time consuming to make that time is wasted that could be spent on actually doing the jobs. Keep preparation simple – the best preparation consists of a balanced life that includes fun, and a good night's sleep.

● Refuse to be a slave to routine – and that includes one imposed by yourself. Question all laws – what are they for? Are they really useful? Kick out all the 'shoulds' and 'oughts' that do not serve a purpose, and be ruthless.

● Look to the future and do not dwell on past mistakes. If you walk backwards, looking towards the past, you will probably fall down a hole. Insist on walking forwards with firm steps. Tomorrow is a new day – the first one of the rest of your life.

● Please take it as read that you can do almost anything, be anyone you choose to be. This is not unrealistic optimism. It is a statement of your inherent ability. Use it well and believe in yourself!

2 Relationships

Hail, wedded Love, mysterious law, true source
Of human offspring

Milton, *Paradise Lost*

It is commonly a weak man, who marries for love

Samuel Johnson

Capricorn has a reputation for being cold, and there is little doubt that Goats are capable of monolithic unresponsiveness when they meet someone they do not like, or of whom they disapprove. Fools are not always suffered gladly, and Capricorn may display all the detachment of Aquarius with rather less of the idealism. However, one of your most deeply buried secrets is that you *can* be idealistic in love. You may cherish the idea of a love, perfect and eternal, through several failed relationships although you may well choose to set this aside and marry 'sensibly'. Feelings are often well concealed, for you may fear to be manipulated, or may not wish to look silly. Extravagant displays are not your style. Believing everyone to be as cynical as your-selves, you fear that emotional expression will look insincere, even when it is deeply felt. However, as you begin to feel more secure, a quaint and charming romanticism peeps out from time to time – but do not hold your breath waiting for this!

Underneath that granite exterior there burns a volcano of emotion and sexual response, and while tightly controlled Capricorn may never erupt, there is likely to be many an earthquake. Secretly, Capricorns yearn for a magical playmate-lover who will lead them deep into the Arcadian forest where their sensual instincts can run wild – and run wild they do, on occasion. However, you often choose partners according to convention and will even endure a loveless relationship for the sake of security and in the cause of duty. Caution and planning figure in Capricornian romance as much as in every other area of life, and there may be an element of the conditional even in your passion.

■ CAPRICORN SEXUALITY

It may come as a surprise to some that Capricorn is one of the most highly sexed signs of the zodiac, vying even with Taurus and Scorpio for the Crown of Horns! As an Earth sign, Capricorn is very much at home with the body. Sexuality is not split from the rest of the personality – Capricornian loins are well connected. Of course, you may choose to file sex under 'pending', but with characteristic thoroughness attention will centre here in the end. Indeed, every ounce of your concentration is given to lovemaking. You are not easily distracted. Nor do you need frills and fantasy – the body of the loved one is enough, and when not harrassed by other demands, Capricorn arousal is swift and straightforward. Sexual fulfilment is important to the Goat, and as with everything else, you believe that 'A thing worth doing is worth doing well'.

Sexually, Ms Capricorn has a long fuse. She is mistress of elegant seduction, and may be well aware that she is 'sitting on a gold mine'. This does not mean that Ms Capricorn cynically exploits her sexuality or sells herself to the highest bidder, but it does mean that she is secure in her body and does not feel that she has to pose and play-act to enhance her appeal. She can be objective. To her, sex doesn't have to mean love. Physical beauty is appealing to her, but she will not be carried away by a pair of biceps, unless it's quite literally, up the stairs.

She is turned on by a fine mind, also. There are, indeed, some Capricorn females who are frigid and guilt-ridden concerning sex, but these are unfortunates whose earthy sensuality has been twisted by a prudish upbringing. The real Ms Capricorn is highly sexed, practised and sensuous, offering a true cornucopia of delights once she has decided to respond.

Mr Capricorn may be a late starter and he may well have read, and memorised several sex manuals before entering the fray. However, because his sexual nature is so basic, there is rarely a wooden quality to his lovemaking. He is in tune with the responses of his lover, and he never pushes the wrong button twice, telling himself 'it said on page ninety-nine that this should work'. His whole body is involved in what he is doing and his partner may be profoundly aware of his masculine strength, which he puts at her service in a way that is quite unforgettable. Capricorn learns quickly in bed, and is deeply gratified by a highly aroused partner as his reward for good performance. Capricorns like to feel secure and usually private when making love. Erotica is often valued, but not essential, and while Capricorns are quite capable of sorties into threesomes and other less orthodox encounters, they generally prefer the stability of a one-to-one partnership. However, a flavour of the illicit is always enticing, so keep a pair of thigh-length boots and a selection of interesting black leather in the wardrobe!

It is true that there is a duality in Capricornian sexuality and many Capricorns never reconcile the need for caution and control with their lusty instincts – and it tends to be the instincts that suffer. Capricorn practicality is too often sidelined into stolidity rather than expressed as sensuality, and it can be a silent tragedy for many Goats that somehow conventionality, in our culture, precludes sexual excitement. Capricorn may dream of being a sinner, but may marry into frustration with a saint. It is a happy Cappy who finds both under the same duvet!

The pipes of Pan

Greek legend tells of Pan, the Goat-Foot God, who despite his half-animal appearance, was irresistibly attractive to the nymphs of wood and mountain. Pan's heart was the heart of the forest and his lust wayward as the wind. And yet, for all his sensual appeal, there was one nymph who shunned him. Her name was Syrinx and Pan loved her with all the passion of his wild nature.

Seeing Syrinx alone one day, Pan approached her, feeling sure that if he could only touch her that she would melt in his arms. However, Syrinx saw him coming and she was overcome by panic. Terrified, she ran – but Pan followed, his heart pounding. Surely her flight meant that she was intent on inflaming his lust! She was heading for the forest, where she would yield to him and he would give her all the love within him. Pan ran after her, and his goat's hooves thudded on the earth.

By a river bank Syrinx stopped, and Pan slowed down. Syrinx raised her arms as if in surrender and Pan gazed in love and desire at her slender form. She was saying something, soft and low. Words of love perhaps, but the sound was as of an incantation. Pan reached for her, expecting her to fall into his embrace – but his eager arms closed on – empty air. There before him, where his beloved had stood, now grew a clump of reeds that sighed forlornly in the breeze.

Pan sat down and hot tears of loss and frustration rolled on to his beard. But sorrow was useless. He must make the best of the situation. The reeds were here, and he could make use of them. Carefully he selected the best of the bunch and bound them into pipes. If he could not be with his love, then he would make music instead. And so Pan walked over the Arcadian hills, playing his pipes and their sad, wild sound became his signature.

Pan displays the lusty, primal side of Capricorn. Syrinx, perhaps, is the fearful, inhibited and prudish side. Most of all this tale tells us of Capricornian pragmatism, for Pan certainly makes the best of a bad job when he turns the remains of his love into a musical instrument. Here is the Capricornian craftsman, who turns feeling into fact. Capricorn may take this as a cautionary tale of what happens when you let your feelings run away with you! However, Pan lives to love another day, and no doubt the mountain nymphs in even greater numbers succumbed to the charms of his unearthly playing.

■ CAPRICORN WOMAN IN LOVE

Ms Capricorn is deeply sensitive, although she will choose to hide her feelings beneath a smooth and cool veneer. She needs security as much as she needs emotional and sexual satisfaction, but she may settle for the former, because it is more reliable, recognisable and easily obtained. She cannot bear continual buffeting in the storms of emotion and may settle this in pragmatic fashion, either by opting for a safe berth from the start or by other strategies. Ms Capricorn is quite capable of coolly running several lovers consecutively, not because she is promiscuous but because she had decided emotional enslavement must not be the order of her life. However, a Capricorn who ties herself to a partner who is safe and dull realises eventually that she has paid a high price and begins to notice the lack of passion and requitement in her secure life.

If Ms Capricorn has decided that her man is the love of her life – and if he also shows signs of being a reasonable companion into the bargain, he should not expect her to throw herself into his arms. He will need patience to win this woman. She will size him up – not judgementally, but practically. She will not be expecting the impossible, and may be realistic about her dreams, she does not want to be let down or taken for a ride, but once she has decided that he is Mr Right, gradually she will bestow all her love, devotion and support. She may never show him her needy side, but it is there and if he can coax it out, or guess at it, deep inside her heart will be warmed. She is much better at giving than taking. Many Capricorn women are endlessly supportive to their chosen mate, making his ambitions their own. She is not a martyr but may willingly sacrifice her own wishes in order to help her mate achieve success – but this should not be carried too far, for Ms Capricorn needs a life of her own and may be extremely frustrated in the end if she tries to live through other people. She may push her lover to achieve for she often has more faith in him than he has in himself – and while she may greet wilder schemes with a discreet cough, she is always there to sort out the practicalities. Adversity brings out the best in her – when the going gets tough, the tough get going. In addition, she is richly sensual, and will often pragmatically adapt to the tastes of her mate, even if dressing up as a French maid does little for her!

Ms Capricorn is often drawn to father figures – which is something of a contradiction, for she is also drawn to the glamourous rebel, whom she feels she can tame. What may happen is that 'father' turns out to have been wild boy all along, and roars off into the sunset astride a Harley Davidson. More happily, in the arms of sensuous Ms Capricorn, Peter Pan may mature enough to come up with the goods. Best of all is when Ms Capricorn expresses her own independence and capability in early life, so she enters relationships with both halves of her – her feminine side and her tough side – well illuminated.

Ms Capricorn hates to see a relationship fail and will try, practically and without apparent emotional excess, to salvage one that hits the rocks. However, she will be deeply hurt inside and it may be a long while before things are the same – if ever they can be. Capricorn is a jealous and possessive sign, slow to trust and often slow to heal.

When Ms Capricorn has chosen her mate he should bask in the gifts of the Earth Goddess and remember that a good harvest means a little dedication and effort. He can see she's worth it.

■ CAPRICORN MAN IN LOVE

The Capricornian male is often an old-fashioned guy, who says little, does lots, and has some true grit in his vitals. The woman this man has chosen should think herself fortunate – or at least complimented – for he has not done it lightly, or in a hurry! With any luck he will take her to a good restaurant, and if she likes it they will go there again . . . and again . . . Capricorn doesn't like change for the sake of it. Nor, usually, will she be expected to pay her way. Of course, once a relationship is established, funds must be discussed and responsibility apportioned. It is a rare Capricorn who doesn't consider financial arrangements as an important part of the package.

A woman should not take it as an insult to her charms if the first date ends with just a peck on the cheek – Mr Capricorn knows the meaning of respect. And if he leaves that warm bed to fill out the mortgage application, it doesn't mean he wouldn't *rather* be in the sack with his lover! It means he's serious! Mr Capricorn would rather act upon his feelings than wallow in the luxury of them, although he may need to be seduced into a little wallowing sometimes, for his own good. Lust is for the beasts and he may rut with the best of them, in season, but love is about commitment and ties, and he's not slow to make them, once his mind's made up. Actions speak louder than words, and his speak volumes, making up for all the times he's too taciturn to say 'I love you'.

Capricorns often do contrive to fall in love with someone they consider an asset. Some Goats take a long time to mature, and while these Kids may make commitments, they are often on the basis of family traditions and pressures. This rarely works. However, the mature Goat is often his own man, and his mate is chosen for different reasons. Perhaps he has recognised that, with her clothes on, she will be a great asset on his arm, at the next company dinner, or maybe her work pays a packet, and Mr Capricorn isn't slow to spot the advantage in that! Of course, there are Capricorns who make meaningless relationships, because they are so inhibited, or crazy Goats who tag along with Miss Dizzy, but mostly there is method in Capricorn love madness, and pragmatism is never too far over the horizon. If nothing else, Capricorn rarely loses sight of how his day-to-day life is going to be and he won't kid himself that he can put up with anything for the sake of love. For instance, had I been a smoker I firmly believe that my Capricorn husband would have remained on visiting terms only!

This guy is a traditionalist, and when a woman has said 'yes' to his proposal she's his and his alone. I have known Capricorns who make like veritable Othellos, but mostly Capricorn has too much common sense for that. However, this man is possessive, jealous and not a little suspicious, although he will usually be too controlled to make this obvious. Some Capricorns can be quite autocratic – Mr Capricorn rules the roost and his job rules him, so if an important dinner has been arranged for his top clients his partner's seminar has to go by the board and she will be expected to occupy herself with the Boeuf en Croute. Worse still, if promotion takes him to the Outer Hebrides, it takes her too, despite her own career – otherwise no relationship. However, such attitudes are in their death throes and many a Capricorn has enough respect for the power of the feminine – to which his Earthy nature gives him access – to respect, support and even delight in his partner's career, and even to sacrifice his own if her earning power is superior. But it is a rare Capricorn whose job is not at least 50 per cent of his life, and at the very least she will need to listen to long accounts of his day at work. This will endear her to him and with any luck she will be treated to some displays of his dry wit, to make it all worthwhile.

For a woman who places a high premium on reliability, security and support, there is no better investment than a commitment to Capricorn. She will need to be a little telepathic on occasion and some-times she will need to be spontaneous enough for two into the bargain. However, it is a great reward to see a spring come into the Goat's step, in spite of himself. Her investment will pay dividends when Interflora brings her twelve red roses on Valentines Day – and she will know that passion's in a pressure cooker perpetually on the back burner and she can turn the heat up any time she wants!

■ GAY CAPRICORN

Because this is such a 'basic' sign, gay Capricorns may well accept their sexuality in a down-to-earth fashion – 'this is what I like, so this is what I am going to do'. Despite the extreme conventionality of many Capricorns, this pragmatism can come to their aid. As we have seen, certain Capricorns are quite happy with their horns and can be wild and sensual – and these are not conventional at all, in most matters! Others will undoubtedly suffer from family condemnation, and will feel bad, if they are male, that they are not carrying on the family name. Females may feel they are failing in their duty to provide grand-children. Duty is often a four-letter word that dogs this sign, and may especially afflict gay Capricorns.

Straight Capricorns may be quite judgemental, for homosexuality can offend their need for everything to be in its correct place and they may not want it 'in their face'. Here the native prudery may surface.

Acceptance should not, in the end, be so difficult for the Goat. After all, nature is as she is, and she is being expressed, not perverted, in homo-sexual love. Conventional Capricorns may like to ask themselves 'Who's making the laws, anyway' and feel happy with their gay acquaintances on the basis that order is certainly being followed.

■ CAPRICORN LOVE TRAPS

Can't buy me love

Despite this sign's reputation, I have never met a mean Capricorn – suspicious, yes, circumspect, undoubtedly – but never mean. However, Capricornian mistrust of life and the human race can lead them to take out a little 'insurance' at times. Saturnian people place little faith in emotions and may sometimes wish to back up their appeal by financial resources. No harm in that you may say – after all, a live-in partnership is a contract and involves money as well as love. That is fine, as far as it goes, but like everything else it needs to be kept in proportion. Some Capricorns evaluate themselves according to their assets – love me, love my car (and house, bank balance, state-of-the-art hi-fi . . .). This doesn't mean that their partners get part shares in all of this. These assets may be displayed like the peacock's feathers – look, but don't touch. Here Capricorn meanness may indeed be discerned, but it comes purely from insecurity. Yours is not a secure, confident sign – although this may be hard to guess. Unsure of your human appeal, you may hope to be loved for your wealth, and yet when you *are* loved for wealth you become suspicious, withholding and resentful. Hardly surprising. The reverse may also be the case, when Capricorn itself is guilty of cupboard love. This all makes for relationships with more cash than care.

Despite all the clichés, money *can* buy you love – but is it the sort of love you want? Definitely not. There is a difference between discussing and arranging money in an upfront fashion in a relationship, and expecting to be fairly treated in this respect, and using money to elicit a pseudo-emotional response. If you recognise yourself in this description, however slightly, do ask yourself why you feel you may not be lovable without your assets. Or, conversely, why you are attracted to wealth in others. What does a relationship truly mean to you? And isn't money something to be arranged together?

Tried and trusted – but not so true

We have mentioned several times that Capricorn in a cautious sign, preferring the 'devil you know' to the one you don't. However, many Capricorns commit themselves to a life of frustration – and often a lingering divorce – through choosing a 'safe' partner. If you are a Capricorn, you are certainly capable of dynamic change – but you will let no one else change you: you have to change yourself. Many Capricorns do change, possibly around the age of thirty, some not until their early forties. It may be hard to imagine this in youth, but it is worth bearing in mind. I'm not trying to change you; I'm not trying to convince you that the reliable option is not for you – it may be. All I am suggesting is some Capricornian caution even in the face of what seems utterly safe. Boredom, restriction, lack of fulfilment – all these are realities in life. You may feel they are inevitable, but they are not, and you can choose a more interesting and rewarding life if you wish. You have the power! So think twice before donning the comfy slippers – those red shoes may fit just as well, and they are made for dancing!

■ CAPRICORN AND MARRIAGE

This sign is generally the 'marrying kind'. All too often Capricorn marries at leisure and repents the same way – for reasons we discussed in the previous section. Choices made when young may be on the basis of family values and are not always to be relied upon. However, yours is a very faithful sign. If you are even moderately happy you are not likely to take time out from the serious business of earning the daily dollar in order to pursue bits on the side. You would far rather get married, consider that area – always a dodgy one – settled, and get on with life.

If things go wrong, Capricorn does not divorce easily. However, yours is not a sign that hangs on through thick and thin. If ignoring the problem does not succeed in making it go away, you will take action. Often when it's over, it's over – no sentimental lingering over love that has died (unless you are still in love, of course). You are quite capable of giving your heart for life, but you are equally capable of marrying without love, and making it work. Although you may succeed in achieving a clean break, yours is a sign that often centres on the past, and while you may have no emotional ties whatsoever remaining to a previous partner, you may still have trouble getting rid of some of the trappings and may drag behind you a trail of useless objects, like a wet tail, convincing yourself they may 'come in handy'. Capricorn doesn't like to be left empty handed!

Capricorns – especially the males – are often dynastically minded. Marriage is for raising families. Of course, this isn't always so, and Capricorn can have an almost idealistic tie to the idea of partnership, that isn't necessarily about emotional closeness. Others are much warmer – almost spontaneous, in fact! – and will marry quickly with the pragmatic (if rather gloomy) view that one might as well enjoy happiness and closeness while one can, because none of us knows when we are going to die! If a marriage does end, Capricorns will shoulder a burden of guilt, if they feel they have been 'to blame'. If not, getting maintenance payments will be like getting blood out of the proverbial stone!

This is a controlling, strong-willed and often moody sign. Those deciding to commit themselves to a Capricorn will need a little toughness and determination to fight – and keep – their corner. Capricorns may need to realise that they cannot control their partners, the household, money, social life (or lack thereof) and Uncle Tom Cobbley and All, – often they will try and it may be a job to wrest the reins from their fists. However, this is not an unreasonable, if stubborn sign, and if partners can give practical reasons for their decisions, so much the better. This notwithstanding,

Capricorn may also have to accept, sometimes, that the partner is doing something 'just because they feel like it.' Capricorns often choose intuitive, emotional partners and then spend their time trying to put their butterflies in boxes. If you are a Capricorn embarking on marriage, remember why you chose this person, don't try to clip his or her wings, and remember that it is quite impractical and inefficient not to share decisions and responsibilities! You don't have to shoulder everything.

■ WHEN LOVE WALKS OUT – HOW CAPRICORN COPES

Forsaken Capricorns usually have their jobs to fall back on and may turn to workaholism rather than alcoholism. Sometimes the Capricorn heart wasn't deeply engaged, in which case time will heal, although scars of mistrust may linger. If Capricorn really was in love, and has now lost, a hard and tragic shell may form as the Goat tells her or himself 'I am a rock, and an island'. But 'no man is an island' and sooner or later, in order to get past this point, Capricorn must let other people close.

Your sign is not always emotionally honest, and sometimes hurt may turn to cold anger and even hatred, which you may deny and yet display in actions that sometimes 'cut off your nose to spite your face', for example. I'd rather be unemployed than pay maintenance to him/her'. At others retaliation will be specific, and ruthless. Not as volatile as Scorpio, you are just as capable of revenge and certainly capable of holding grudges. When hurt, the cruel streak of which you are sometimes accused, can surface and you may feel satisfaction in the distress of the former partner. Friends may need to be very patient for you may push people away – but company and support are obviously needed. Friends should not expect you to cry on their shoulders – it's not your style. However, if you can be induced to talk it will help. You may need to turn yourself around, stop looking at the past and harness that pragmatism to walk steadily into the future.

Starting afresh

The danger is that you may decide not to. 'Once bitten, twice shy.' But some Goats hit a 'giddy' phase and may kick up their heels in their own special Saturnalia. What you need to retrieve is your trust in life, and as you never had much of it in the first place this may be difficult. Capricorn is capable of loving 'on the rebound' but you are far more likely to go into your own private cave. It is fine to wait and to mourn – but this should be mourning, not calcifying. The whole point is to transform, not to go into permanent chrysalis mode. So you can turn perhaps to work and career for a while and bolster your confidence in this area. In general, a practical project, where there can be real, tangible results as a reward, is recommended and so fortified by some solid achievement, the Goat can go forward. Although some Goats do become perpetually embittered and pessimistic, others gain strength from having survived and coped and actually feel more confident of starting another relationship because of this – and then do so from a much sounder basis.

■ PRACTICE AND CHANGE ■

- Practise expressing your sincere feelings. As long as it is truthful, there is no need to feel silly. This will not make your relationship frivolous – it will make it more gratifying and stable.

- Caution may cheat you of fulfilment. A safe choice can become a prison, keeping you from emotional and sexual gratification.

- If you are a 'prudish' Capricorn, ask yourself why. Where is it written that you should not kick up your hooves once in a while?

- In relationships you need to take as well as give. By this I mean that both you and your partner will be gratified if he or she can help you, instead of the other way round.

- If you are prone to evaluate yourself on the basis of your assets, this is coming not from practicality but insecurity. Try to learn to value yourself for what you are, not for what you have. And if you aren't sure what you are, set yourself the task of finding out!

- Take the time to develop your own values. You may well have swallowed whole the conventions of your upbringing. Is this best for you and your relationships?

- Remember that in a committed relationship you cannot keep control of everything. Your relationship will be much smoother and more satisfying if power is shared.

- If a relationship has ended you must walk forwards in a way that is most beneficial to you. Resentments are bad for the digestion – be too practical to entertain them. It may be hard to trust in the future, but you can make something out of it on the basis of what you have learnt, and find yourself on a sounder footing than before.

3 All in the family

I was ever of opinion that the honest man who married and brought up a large family, did more service than he who continued single and only talked of population.

Oliver Goldsmith, *The Vicar of Wakefield*

Capricorns usually have a strong sense of family and the structure of the household. You usually like to uphold routines, and can be relied upon to shut windows, lock doors and adjust clocks. You do not take kindly to changes in habits and although co-operative for the most part, you can be quite autocratic when your schedules are interfered with.

■ CAPRICORN MOTHER

It is often said that Capricorn is the 'sign of the father' which may make Ms Capricorn sound masculine, stern and authoritative. While the last two adjectives may apply, and while it is usual for Capricorn to be strong and independent, Capricorn mother is definitely all woman, and a very maternal one. Our concept of the 'feminine' tends to be rather fluffy and yielding. In the ancient mystical doctrine of the Qabalah, Binah, the Supernal Mother on the Tree of Life, equates with Saturn. So our 'patriarch' is in a sense Earth Mother, bringing qualities of firmness and authority to the feminine. Many people believe that rulership was held by women in the distant past, and certainly there is much that is quietly commanding about Ms Capricorn.

This lady must 'climb' herself, or she will do it vicariously, driving her loved ones to achievements they may not wish for themselves and thus courting resentment. Because she tends to the conventional, Capricorn mother might, until recent years, have shelved ideas of a career for herself in order to devote herself to her family. Big mistake! This lady is a much better and more relaxed mum if her ambitions are fulfilled, and she is usually extremely capable of running a household, bringing up children and achieving in the workplace, also. Her efficiency is often staggering and she may well deserve the title Superwoman of the zodiac, for she does not waste energy. The only drawback may be that she underestimates her capability and resources and says 'no' when she could say 'yes'. She needs to make time for treats, outings and relaxation, whatever her commitments.

Capricorn mother likes her children to be a credit to her and will delight in hearing of their achievements. She may turn a little deaf to whingeing and worrying. This isn't because she doesn't care, because she does – deeply. However, she wants her offspring to achieve the same tight emotional control that she has – because this is a hard world, and it is harder on those who haven't developed a thick hide. In this she needs to remind herself that, far from making a child weak, in the long run children are strengthened through having complete emotional support. With this inner warmth in place they can brave the icy winds of life undaunted, shrugging off the times when they are rejected and hurt because they know they are 'okay'. Capricorn mother rarely trusts life and desperately wants to protect her little ones from injury. She may instill in them fear and mistrust, feeling it is their best defence, conscious of her own limitations in keeping them from harm. In this she underestimates her own power. Her love can shield them and her gift of common sense is their most effective weapon.

Thrift is important to Capricorn mother and she probably will not be lavish, even when she can afford to be. Capricorns rarely see life as generous and want their children to be able to manage and provide for themselves. Capricorns often adhere to social mores, but as these become more relaxed so does Capricorn – although she may be the last one on the block to make it into the twenty-first century! Capricorn is artistic and creative, and this mother encourages her children to put their ideas into practice. She may be a bit of a hard task-master, but she has a soft centre and her puckish sense of humour can often be appealed to. Her children shouldn't be afraid to pay her compliments or to say they love her – she may look all stiff and disapproving but inside her heart is glowing.

■ CAPRICORN FATHER

Capricorn dad is a true 'paterfamilias' taking his place at the head of the table as to the manor born. This is a dynastic sign, and Capricorn men love to have sons 'to carry on the family name'. Of course, they will love their daughters equally, but somehow they feel they have done their duty if they have produced a boy. Capricorns are eager to see that their children get the best education possible; this is likely to be of a conventional mode.

Capricorn father is often absent because he tends to spend so much time at work. He's generally not all that good at playing with the children either and may have to be coaxed into joining the family on outings. However, his sense of responsibility can usually be appealed to, and if it is explained to him that it is his duty – that word again! – to devote time to the children, he will comply. In general it is much better if Capricorn dad can take the little ones into his world, in some shape or form – children actually love that. Going to dad's office or sitting behind the wheel of his truck can be ecstasy.

This dad is better at helping his kids grow up than enjoying their childhood, and he must be careful he doesn't try to put an old head on young shoulders. He can be stern and inflexible, rather addicted to the letter of the law. However, he usually respects toughness in his kids 'because it stands them in good stead later on'. In fatherhood, as in so many respects, Capricorn improves with age, and Capricorn dad in his late thirties may be more indulgent than one adapting to the responsibilities of parenthood in his twenties.

Occasionally Mr Capricorn resents his children – remember old Cronos, who swallowed them all? This is a jealous sign, and he may feel the affections of his wife have been usurped. Not being a demanding or demonstrative character, Capricorn will probably not deal with this situation, but will tell himself sternly to 'grow up' – or not even recognise the feelings are present, so execrable does he find them. However, he will then take out his feelings on the children by being harsh and punitive. Capricorn, rarely a spontaneous sign, may simply resent the vitality and carefree zest for life his children enjoy – especially if they are Fire signs. He may then crush this in his children. This is a great shame. A Capricorn dad can gain so much from the pleasures of a child and may find that youth he was never quite sure he had in the company of youngsters. If Capricorn can add to his protective and formative qualities a little laughter and playfulness, fatherhood can make his life complete.

■ THE CAPRICORN CHILD

The Capricorn child is serious, studious and dutiful. She or he may have a talent for making the parents feel frivolous. Young Capricorns need routines and will feel quite put out if they are disturbed. Capricorns will create their own order and may be outraged if toys are not found in their allocated places. This is not a child to have tantrums, unless there is a strong Fire or Water content somewhere in the chart, and Capricorn isn't given to open defiance. However, if Capricorns want something, they are not to be diverted and their parents may find they have got their own way in the end – a sign of things to come! This child, with reasonable encourage-ment, is going somewhere in life. Not quickly, but inexorably.

Most Capricorns will do their homework before going out to play – if they go out to play at all. Young Capricorns love to be around adults and many choose friends who are several years older than they are. Capricorns are often artistic and creative – they love to make things and see you use them. Don't worry if this child seems too studious and quiet – it doesn't mean he or she is 'maladjusted'. Encourage Capricorns gently to loosen up or go out, but *never* make them feel guilty (this is all too easy with Capricorn). It is quite natural to them to be reserved, and they are enjoying life in their own way.

Adolescence can be painful for Capricorns because teenage rebel-lion just isn't their style and they may not know how to 'hang out' with the gang, so they may feel outcast. Along with the strong sexual urges that are now emerging, life can be hell. Capricorns want to initiate contact with the opposite sex, but their formality makes them middle-aged in approach, and others may laugh at them. Capricorn girls are often more fortunate here than the boys, for their reserve can make them very seductive. However, Capricorns often elicit respect for being their 'own person', and with their grit-ty practicality they are capable of acquiring 'street wisdom'. Despite their characteristic stiffness, Capricorns can be early starters with sex, and may even wish to commit to marriage by sixteen. Capricorns are very conscious of the 'march of time' and may even fear being left on the shelf! Parents should take this seriously – Capricorn does. All this should be talked out adult to adult, and while, naturally, most parents will hope against hope that Capricorn will grow out of it, opposition is definitely counter-productive, because the Goat's hooves will simply dig in deeper. However, an adolescent is an adolescent even when born under Capricorn, and buying a little time is always desirable. If not, be at hand to pick up the pieces. Capricorn will learn from mistakes.

Having said all of this, there is a type of Capricorn who refuses to grow up, who does raise veritable hell, and who slouches into early adulthood resentful, pessimistic and uncooperative. Capricorn is a strong sign, and such a one can make parents' lives an utter misery for a while – but not for ever.

Capricorn often pays in advance, in youthful sobriety, to buy a light-hearted middle age. When parents are in their bath chairs, their Capricorn sons or daughters may well be at their best – helpful, attentive, respectful and entertaining.

■ CAPRICORN AS SIBLINGS

As an older sibling Capricorn will in all probability be like another parent, which can be good or bad, depending how you look at it. As early as possible Capricorn will babysit – and will expect to be paid for it! A Capricorn older brother or sister is often protective and helpful, but may be cutting or scornful about failures and imperfections. Capricorn cruelty can surface on occasion. If Capricorn is the younger one, she or he will often study carefully the ways of the elder and will emulate, where suitable. Often Capricorn hangs around elders more like a sheep than a goat, but if the 'big ones' transgress, Capricorn cannot be trusted to keep the secret! Liking approval and respecting authority, little Capricorn may well tell tales. If other siblings are mean to Capricorn he or she can plot their come-uppance with all the vengefulness of Scorpio, but often in such a subtle way they can never prove anything! This is definitely a brother or sister to keep on the right side of because, sure as eggs is eggs, Capricorn will be useful to them some day. As time goes by siblings will become closer – Capricorns, like good wine, improve with age, and no one will reminisce with you about the good old days with quite the moist-eyed twinkle of Capricorn.

■ CAPRICORN IN THE HOME

Pragmatic Capricorns usually adapt quite well to prevailing conditions and often they are instinctive about keeping their possessions orderly. Capricorns have sound ideas about how to use space to the best advantage and will be making the best of what is available anyway. Thus, if it suits Capricorns to hang their clothes from a picture hook, how it looks may not matter that much to them. Some Capricorns are prepared to spend hours fiddling with their possessions, preparing, sorting and getting things from the back of the cupboard for the following day, and will take it as their lot, in this vale of tears, to cope with pokey conditions! Others won't bother, and will accept living in a heap, as long as what is around them is useful. Most difficult of all, some Capricorns are so addicted to the past that they won't throw anything out and will convince themselves that even a broken shoelace will come in handy – and knowing them, it will! The best approach is to have blitzes while Capricorn is out – I know it sounds dishonest, but Capricorns usually will grudgingly acceed to common sense. It is advisable simply to restrict Capricorn space, and return possessions firmly to home base in bedroom or on desk. Capricorn will usually manage to find a slot.

■ PRACTICE AND CHANGE ■

- To be dutiful is laudable, and no one would wish to change this in you. But duty, as a parent, is not the whole story. Joy, too has a place. You know it is your *duty* to enjoy your children! Don't forget it!

- Children are given a fund of strength by being loaded with love. Do not be afraid to indulge your love for your children, to allow them close and to be warm. This will not make them vulnerable. Love is the best insurance policy going – take it out and pay the premiums.

- If your Capricorn child is quiet and studious, think your-self lucky, and do not worry that he or she is a social misfit. Respect their ways and they will learn self-respect.

- Of course, not all Capricorn children are introverts. If your young Capricorn is a tearaway try to console yourself with the belief he or she is rebelling against life (which seems arduous) not against you.

- Because Capricorn tends to be 'sensible' one should not forget that this is a creative sign. Capricorns should have opportunity in the home to express this.

- It is a rare Capricorn who does not need routines. More laid-back parents may need to make an effort to provide routines for young Capricorn. Older Capricorns can be an asset to the family by keeping younger members orderly, but should not impose meaningless schedules on others simply so they can feel more secure.

- With Capricorn, so much improves with age. Give Capricorns encouragement – but no coercion – to change themselves. Given time they often do.

4 Friendships and the single life

To have what we want is riches; but to be able to do without is power

George Macdonald

Friendships are naturally important to us all, whether we are married or single. However, single people often have more time to spend with their friends. With Capricorn, it may be difficult enough finding time for the steady partner in a busy work schedule, and so friends may receive even less attention from Capricorns with partners. However, this isn't always the case. Capricorn is a faithful sign and the past is not readily left behind – thus, Capricorns will often maintain relationships for years, even though communication may be slender, and they will be there for their old friends, if needed.

■ CAPRICORN AS A FRIEND

Capricorns like to give practical help and sound advice. If friends are moving house you will help them pack the boxes and if they need advice to end a relationship, you will point them in the direction of a good solicitor. Emotional support is not Capricorn's strong suit. If friends tell you they are worried about their wrinkles, you may refer them to the latest dermatological treatment or discuss the pros and cons of facelifts. You are unlikely to say 'What, you? Wrinkled! I would never have noticed' or to tell them that they look years younger than they are. To a Capricorn that might smack of effusiveness or insincerity, and you would far rather give them a direction in which to act than soothe their worries. After all, such blandishments would not work with you Capricorns – you would generally far rather know how to act upon a problem than be convinced it didn't exist. However, some problems *don't* exist – they are imaginary, growing from lack of self-esteem. It will do you no harm at all to hear when you are being pessimistic – for the Capricornian bottle is always half empty, never half full. At such times a hefty dose of positive realism coupled with a sincere, muted compliment, can warm you inside and make your ears turn pink.

Capricorns are quite capable of being friends for life. You do not give your trust easily, but once given you are reliable. However, should friends betray your trust, they should not expect to be given a second chance, for you are capable of completely cutting off a friendship and won't be taken for a ride twice. If friends let you down, they merely confirm your suspicion that life is hell bent on catching you out. After that experience you may be slower to trust everyone: you certainly won't make the same mistake again. Occasionally there are cynical Capricorns who are capable of using people, and it is true that Capricorn is quite capable of picking friends who can ease the climb up the social ladder or aid advancement at work. However, mostly these reserved people have a rich fund of companionship and affection; 'cold hands, warm heart' can apply, metaphorically, to the Goat.

Many Capricorns find their principal source of friendships at work or while pursuing an interest, and they often like to have friends with whom they can discuss the burning issues. This is partly because we form relationships largely on the basis of interests, and Capricorns are usually very interested in their work. But it is also an instinctive device to fend off closeness. Capricorns fear dependence, fear being too close to another because of loss of autonomy or power. Because of this they may prefer to give, to help and to listen rather than to take, be helped or pour out their troubles. It may be hard for friends to get to know you, or you may make them feel a little inadequate through your self-sufficiency. You do not like to burden people with your problems – although there are a few Capricorn miseries, who make an artform out of self-pity, but these are a rarity, and it is sometimes doubtful whether they *want* to be cheered up!

Self-sufficient Capricorn can be a strengthening influence to be close to. Often you are best left alone when depressed, but not for too long, for eventually you climb out of the pit and get on with life. However, friends should not be put off by your curt answers when in the doldrums – their concern is appreciated, although they might never guess it, and although their care may remain unacknowledged it will not be forgotten.

■ CAPRICORN AND THE SINGLE LIFE

The Goat often copes very well with being single and may even appear to embrace it on purpose, possibly to prove a point. It is often far more important to you to show you can do without anyone than to prove you are popular and sociable. To Capricorn there is no shame in being solitary. Home can be a castle and a bastion. If you have contact with people at work you may be happy with almost no social life.

However, the Earth Element needs physical contact, and there are Capricorns who are conscious of being extremely unhappy when alone, and this may become more evident as Capricorn matures. Lonely Capricorns can disappear inside themselves. This is a sign that generally needs to be 'out there' making some sort of difference in the world. Of course, some people are deeply introverted, and have little need for friends, but if this is the case, there should usually be a purpose to the solitary state. How is time alone being used? Is it gainfully employed? Are solitary pursuits a genuine source of joy? Or is there a certain amount of miserable moping and inward 'maggotting'? Capricorns who live alone may immerse themselves in work, spending far longer than they need to at the office.

It is important to you to ask yourself what you are trying to prove. Is time alone being used to compensate for resentments, or punitively, on the lines of 'The world's always been unkind to me, so I'll show them all – I'll keep away from them'. Again, this is cutting off one's nose to spite one's face. Longer hours should not be worked for the sake of it. Capricorn is an achieving sign, and the question must always be asked 'Where is this leading me?' Capricorns whose relationships continually founder because they can't, or won't get close again need to ask themselves what they are trying to prove, where, and why, have they learnt not to trust, and what they are going to do about it?

Capricorns who genuinely like being alone may use this time to probe deep into the mysteries of systems like the mystical Jewish Qabalah, Earth Mysteries, meditation – or, indeed, any esoteric subject to which Capricorn can apply the approach of the realist and pragmatist, the achiever and the expert. Capricorn, although often interested in the arcane, likes practical results and identifiable conclusions, and thus is often systematic, painstaking and very authoritative. Again, this sign is 'making a difference' and if that difference is internal, it is no less real. Sometimes only by bringing about real change within can anything notable be wrought externally. While Capricorns may be well-nigh impossible to change, they are capable of radically changing themselves.

■ PRACTICE AND CHANGE ■

- Make space in your life for friends. At some time you may feel you need friends, so think of this as an insurance policy for the future. Make a social life part of your schedule.

- If you are a Capricorn who sees friends as a means to an end, in career or status terms, you are missing out on a great deal. What is this all about? Human warmth needs to be part of your value system, also.

- Remember friends do not always want practical help. It can be a drag if they merely want to unburden themselves and you are trying to sort it all out for them. There is great value in just listening.

- We are all human so don't be too harsh on a good friend on the basis of one lapse. Think of all the good things about this person – that is worth a lot.

- Letting people close can be a sign of strength, not vulnerability – and friends can make you stronger. Have faith in your ability to recover from possible disappointments and to cope.

- In your case 'It is more blessed to give than to receive' needs to be turned about. Give other people the 'blessing' of letting them help, once in a while.

- If you have chosen to be alone, how are you spending your time? Are you really enjoying it/using it constructively? If the answer to this is 'No' in both cases then why are you alone? Is there not something you could do about this?

- If you are a Capricorn who wants to relate yet is too shy, lacking in confidence or feeling 'unlikeable' this is where you need to call on your native pragmatism and common sense. Look for groups where you can *do* something together, and where your input can be appreciated for its own sake – you don't have to be the life and soul of the party.

5

Career

*Genius is one per cent inspiration and
ninety-nine per cent perspiration*

Thomas Edison

Moving on to the subject of career for Capricorn, now we are really talking! It is a rare Capricorn for whom career is not of prime importance and it could be said that many Capricorns live to work, not work to live. Of course, this isn't always to be recommended, on health grounds if nothing else. However, many Capricorns find true self-expression in their work, and every effort should be made to secure an occupation that is fulfilling – otherwise it's a miserable Goat!

We know there are 'Giddy Goats' and these may seem to be more irresponsible than the most flagrant Sagittarian. However, sooner or later it is deeply important to Capricorns to find a niche in society and a place where they can make a noticeable difference: Capricorns are made to make their mark.

■ TRADITIONAL CAPRICORN CAREERS

The common denominator for all occupations suitable for Capricorns is that they involve some degree of attention to structure, planning and control. Capricorn careers include:

- mathematician
- osteopath
- scientist
- teacher
- civil servant
- politician
- engineer
- farmer

- builder
- musician
- architect
- surveyor
- administrator
- businessperson
- mineralogist
- sculptor
- cartographer
- dentist
- manager

■ WHAT TO LOOK FOR IN YOUR WORK

The great majority of people work in large insurance corporations, sales offices, shops, banks and factories. Relatively few of us can choose a profession, train for it and find a fulfilling lifestyle, and as time progresses this is becoming more elusive.

To help you find a job that suits you, you need to bear in mind the spirit of what is recommended, not the specific occupation. One office job is not like another, one shop selling fashions may differ enormously from one down the street in terms of environment and opportunity. As a Capricorn you need to make sure of several things when seeking employment:

- You have as much security of employment as it is possible to find.
- You have clearly defined contract, hours of work, job definition, etc.
- There is scope for you to advance within the existing structure.
- You have, or have the prospect of earning, control of your own work schedule.
- While you probably do not have a problem with authority, you will prefer not to have anyone breathing down your neck.
- Money should be good, and rising.
- You will like it best if you respect your boss and can regard her or him as a mother or father figure or mentor, to some extent.

- You will need to feel appreciated – although it is most unlikely that you will show this. You also like to feel you are making a real difference.
- Some Capricorns like to travel, but many do not! You are not likely to adapt to a job that takes you to far-flung parts at a moment's notice unless your chart has plenty of Fire or Air to balance the Capricorn. If you are called upon to travel, you will like time to prepare and to know what you are facing.

From this you can see that there is no need to feel that you have to look for a specifically Capricornian job. Many Capricorns would be mystified by osteopathy or bored to death on a farm. Look for something that suits in its content and atmosphere rather than its label. If it isn't right, plan carefully and make changes.

■ ALL THE HOURS GOD SENDS

Capricorn is probably the workaholic of the zodiac, challenged in this only by Virgo. Many Capricorns are afraid not to be needed. In all fairness, many Capricorns equally place themselves in such a position that the organisation could well collapse without them, for they are not good at delegating. 'All the hours God sends' are spent at the desk with forehead crumpled and pile of work already completed at the time when all the rest stagger in and head for the coffee machine. Capricorn is still there when everyone goes home. Many Capricorns are quite capable of camping out at the office for days – but these are usually executives. 'All-the-hours' is heading for executive status, that is if he or she doesn't drop dead on the way!

This person is always one jump ahead and has the knack of making others feel guilty and inferior. 'All-the-hours' is ostensibly working for advancement, or for a retirement that may never come. Needless to say, this person almost definitely has an impoverished homelife. While 'All-the-hours' probably achieves a measure of advancement, this is not the high-flying Capricorn, but rather one who has tethered themselves to some imaginary post. What they are really afraid of is that emotional void that would await them out in the green fields of freedom and opportunity. Now, if this is you, you are under-selling yourself. You are probably too tired, or have developed career myopia, through excessive concentration on doing anything and everything as well as you can. Excellence in the trivial is a waste of time and energy. A thing worth doing is sometimes worth doing badly if it frees you to do something more important – something that gets you on in life. What is there to be afraid of? You are on a treadmill. What opportunities are you missing, going round and round and round . . . ? There are other paths available for you in life and you are selling yourself short. Get a life. Look up at the peaks and start to climb.

■ THE CLIMBER

In the Climber we meet the true Capricorn, expressing much of the virtue and some of the vices of the sign. These people are often unobstrusive early in their career. They are waiting, watching and learning. Mostly they are in the right place at the right time, hand extended dutifully, to take the visiting executive's coat and hang it carefully on a hanger. Climber wears just the right things, usually of impeccable quality and cut. Choice of watch or jewellery will display good taste, but never the flashy. This person is reliable, well informed and hard working, but has more sense than to strain those clear eyes burning the midnight oil. Climber realises that everything has value, everything is an investment, including health, alertness and vitality, and apportions time intelligently. Yes, these people are often called 'crawler', or worse, and their pride can sometimes be supple when it comes to pleasing the right person.

They are often calculating and opportunistic. But everything is done for a purpose, and judiciously. Climber is rarely called 'arse-licker' by those who matter. She or he will more likely be called 'efficient, helpful, reliable, indispensible – a jewel'.

You can't knock this. Climber is going places, going to the top by a circuitous route, but a sure one. No short cuts, just the best way forwards and upwards. Others who value their own future should keep on the right side of Climber, whatever it costs them. Climber is Capricorn at her or his best, in the best Capricornian arena. Sooner or later this person is going to make a difference.

■ THE CAPRICORN BOSS

Being a boss is a natural position for Capricorn, and it is a rare Goat who does not attain some form of authority or influence. This person often makes a home out of office or car, and may bring personal paraphernalia to work, if space permits. Yes, sometimes Capricorn boss will sleep at the office, but will have no intention of being uncomfortable. Capricorn boss loves work and will expect the same from employees. They are not susceptible to charm and if employees have made a mistake, they should admit and rectify it *at once*. Capricorn is looking for one thing and one thing alone – results. And this person wants dedication: there is no place for 'jobsworths'. Employees do their best and if they've finished ahead of schedule they should look for other work that needs doing – like Capricorn did on the way up. If they are found wanting, Capricorn will get rid of them, either by leaning steadily on them until they break or finding some contractual loophole. Capricorn boss is determined, patient and resourceful. Employees won't outlast or out-think this boss, if he or she has the bit between the teeth. Capricorn boss can be nasty!

Before employees check their boss's birthdate and run screaming for the Jobcentre, they should remember this. Capricorn boss is horrid when bad, but when good is very, very good indeed. There is a sensitive side to Capricorn – these efficient people are often lacking in confidence and inner security, and if Capricorn is sure of employees' loyalty he or she will respond to their needs like an indulgent parent. 'No, you can't have time off to buy a late birthday present', but 'of course you can be away to look after an ageing parent' or to cope with depression. Capricorn often understands that all too well. This boss is realistic and often sympathetic, but will certainly be suspicious of frequent 'convenient' illnesses. Office clowns and bright sparks will get short shrift. At the office party, Capricorn boss will organise and dispense drinks with efficiency and often an indulgent smile, rather like a parent at a kid's birthday party. However, only the giddiest of Goats will get caught cavorting with a lampshade on their heads, or in the corridor with the office junior. Of course, some Capricorn bosses are certainly capable of disappearing for an hour . . . However, Capricorn will appear again, in due course, with a bland expression and not a hair out of place. Capricorn bosses don't need an excuse – who would dare to challenge them?

Employees should be respectful to their Capricorn boss, be reliable, should not pilfer or talk to friends and family on the office phone. If they keep away from him or her when a fit of the grumps hit, it will go away in due course. They should pay their boss a quiet compliment – but make sure it's sincere, and don't expect an immediate smile in response. Capricorn boss expects them to have a hidden agenda. Just don't let it get out of hand. Decent and non-challenging employees will eventually be treated to the consideration, quiet charm and understated humour of requited Capricorn. It will warm their hearts – and, with any luck, their pockets.

■ THE CAPRICORN EMPLOYEE

Employers shouldn't let this person's obsequious attitude and undemanding presence deceive them: they may be in the presence of a climbing Goat. Capricorn employee probably had the company thoroughly checked out before honouring it with her or his presence. Capricorn often comes in early, goes home late, and has a stock of fine biros that never run out of ink.

Not all Capricorns are this smooth, however. Some Goats-in-the-making have all the presence of A. A. Milne's Eeyore with his collapsed balloon. Often these Capricorns start out with the acceptance that life is a pile of rubble stacked in their way, but as they begin to clear it, slowly their self-esteem mounts. Goats rarely enter into the office badinage, but when they do they utter a quiet witticism that floors everyone. Slowly Capricorn comes to earn everyone's respect, charming the cleaner and the MD.

Capricorn employees need to be appreciated. They may not make a bid for centre stage and colleagues may think they continue, unflagging, whatever the conditions. They do, usually, but they are not firing on all cylinders if they feel their best efforts are passing unnoticed. Capricorn employees are resourceful and often have the company interests at heart, which they see as their interests also. Through observation and practicality this employee can come up with some workable and helpful ideas. Capricorns have little patience with systems that don't work, and don't suffer fools gladly, although this will remain concealed until Capricorn is in a position to do something about it. Send Capricorns home if they work late too many nights on the trot. Compliment this person in season, raise her or his salary when you can and do promote when possible. This is just about the most valuable employee you can get, but despite the biddable exterior, Capricorn will eventually leave if dissatisfied. Don't let that happen!

■ WHEN UNEMPLOYMENT STRIKES

Capricorn is often lost without work and the sad stories of people who get up, dress for the office and are gone all day for months, or even years, after their positions have been terminated, may well be Capricorns, trying to convince themselves as much as their families that they have a purpose in life. Having said this, many Capricorns do adapt to unemployment with characteristic pragmatism. How well Capricorns cope will depend how far they have proved themselves. If Capricorns feel confident they have a talent to sell, they will go about doing this in the most efficient way possible.

It is most important that Capricorn does not succumb to depression when out of work. To avoid this the routine should continue as much like before as possible – up at the same time, dress smartly and find something important to do. Turn looking for a job into a job, and plan time including lunchbreaks. Put in exactly the time you would have formerly spent at your old job. Do not deviate from this, except for important events. There are certainly times in life when Capricorn needs to slow down and take a holiday, but this is not one of them. Momentum should be maintained. It is your duty and your purpose to find another niche. If you are not sure whether you want a change of direction, spend time in finding out what is available, not in kicking your heels. This may seem like a pit, but grit your teeth. You will get out of it.

■ SELF-EMPLOYMENT AND OTHER MATTERS

Capricorn is fairly well suited to self-employment, but may first prefer to get the experience and confidence that comes from working within a tried-and-tested system. This is a Cardinal sign, and as such often dynamic and self-starting. Goats are also self-disciplined and usually excellent planners of time and money. The only small drawback can occasionally be that some Goats – but not all – may lack flexibility and imagination. This could be supplied by the right partner.

■ PRACTICE AND CHANGE ■

- In your work you need security, well-defined objectives, reasonable money and prospects of advancement. If you do not feel satisfied, take steps to find a new job.

- Do not convince yourself that you do not need pats on the back. You do. Look for a position or boss that supplies appreciation of your achievements.

- If your present job is unsatisfactory but takes too much of your time and energy for you to be able to look for another job, then you must *make time*, before you get too depressed and disheartened.

- Be honest – are you over-working, convincing yourself that you are useful, even indispensable, but going nowhere? Facing this now is better than to have the realisation forced on you, ten or twenty years in the future, when you will be able to do nothing about it.

- We know your work is important to you, but it also can mean no meaningful family life, romance or fun. All these are very important. Be sensible, realise this and make room for them.

- Goats often find it hard to delegate, but if you are ambitious this is something you will have to learn.

- You may be one of those rare Goats who doesn't take much interest in work, but Capricorn usually has a purpose in life – maybe yours is about educating yourself, being creative and artistic or looking after others – or maybe it is more esoteric. Whatever the case, it is sure to be taking you somewhere!

---

6 Healthy, wealthy – and wise?

Better put a strong fence around the top of the cliff,
Than an ambulance down in the valley

Joseph Malines

■ HEALTH

Astrological reflections on health are sometimes of doubtful help
or accuracy, because health is dependent on so many factors. What
might we usefully say about the health of Capricorns in general?

The Capricorn constitution is generally sound, and this is reputed
to be a long-lived sign. Because of the rather controlled nature of
many Capricorns, nothing is done to excess, and this can make for
a sensible, balanced lifestyle. Capricorn is not prone to 'forget' the
body, like some of the more abstract signs. Physical health, reasonable meals and exercise, if there is time, are things that Capricorn is
likely to regard as important, and to attend to. As this is a rather
conventional sign, faddy diets are not often adopted, and there may
be an old-fashioned adherence to 'meat-and-two-veg'. However, this
is by no means always the case, for there sometimes surfaces an
imaginative and exploratory streak in Capricorn – and as we saw in
earlier chapters the 'saturnalian' aspect may take over, indicating a
Capricorn who adopts excess in almost anything!

Health problems are most likely to surface in Capricorn through
overwork. This can be as a direct result of the stresses of the work
itself, or because work does not leave enough time to attend to
health matters. Thus, the Goat may suffer from conditions like a

bad back, eye strain and fatigue (although Capricorn doesn't generally tire easily) or there may be simply too much time spent at a desk,
with all its attendant problems. Capricorns can be great worriers – it
is as if Capricorn cannot be content without a certain level of misery!
In addition, emotions are often suppressed. Capricorn may also be
prone to depression and generally a pessimistic outlook. This may
result in a clinical condition, requiring anti-depressants or may be
the underlying cause of persistent colds, headaches, etc. Generally,
Capricorns suffering from minor problems – or even major ones –
would be well advised to examine first the demands of their workload
and their attitude to it as a possible influencing factor. Of course, this
applies to many people and not just to Capricorn, but of all the signs
Capricorn is a great one for working too hard, for too long.

Being great stoics, Capricorns often take the attitude that they must
shoulder burdens and not complain. There is nothing to be gained
by this approach, which is hardly realistic. If there are health problems, small or large, professional medical advice should be sought.
To believe that nothing can be done to help is to buy into the belief
that life is against one, and health is one of the areas where such an
attitude can be a self-fulfilling prophecy.

Skin and bones

Capricorn is said to rule the knees. It is also linked to the structural
components of the body, namely the skeleton and the skin. The skin
forms the outer boundary of the body, and 'boundaries' are a
Capricornian motif. Some Capricorns may find they are especially
prone to rashes and skin complaints, when under the weather, and
this is, of course, the body's way of eliminating harmful factors.
However, equally many Capricorns have clear, perfect skin, as if the
epidermis itself were co-operating in the attempt to live a controlled
and orderly existence!

The knees are an interesting connection, for we speak of being 'brought to our knees' by life's burdens. This is how some Capricorns feel. Nature being a complex and wonderful thing, it is interesting how often physical complaints are a metaphor for psychological states. Louise Hay, author of *You Can Heal Your Life* relates knee problems to 'stubborn ego and pride. Inability to bend. Fear. Inflexibility. Won't give in', Capricorns with problems in the knees may find it helpful to ask themselves where, in life, these factors apply. Sometimes we have become so used to behaving in a certain way, we fail even to consider another – we do not recognise that we are being 'inflexible', we just assume that's the way to be, that is the way we have always been.

Back and shoulder problems, arthritis and aches and pains in any part of the skeletal structure may also affect Capricorn, for reasons given above. Dancing may be a help, providing exercise, loosening up and creative movement in a therapeutic and pleasurable package. Capricorn is prone to believe that if it doesn't taste bad or feel unpleasant then it can't be doing any good! Nothing could be further from the truth and many Capricorns would enjoy better health if they learnt the value of pleasure.

■ MONEY

Not to put too fine a point on it, this sign has a reputation for being a skinflint. Dickens' Scrooge displays many of the Capricornian traits, ranging from outright meanness to paternal benevolence in the course of *A Christmas Carol*. Equally, with the occasional ambiguity of the sign, the Goat can be very generous. In this case it is a heart-warming trait, for it arises from knowledge of the value of things, a true assessment of priority, rather than the impulsiveness or lack of realism of some signs who are more known for generosity.

And yes, there are even extravagant Capricorns, who live on credit, every so often having attacks of extreme parsimony, but returning to the plastic in the knowledge and belief that they can 'manage' it. As long as Capricorns can service debts, month by month, they may be able to cope. Occasionally, the more opportunistic and less principled Capricorn may turn to devious ways of making a buck – Capricorn likes to cut a smart figure, and this costs money. However, the majority of Capricorns, with their penchant for the respectable, would lose many hours of sleep at the mere suggestion of anything nefarious.

Although the Capricornian habit of weighing everything up is laudable, it isn't everything. As with so many other spheres of life, the control that one can take is limited. Capricorn must learn that sensible safeguards and precautions are commendable, and necessary, obsession and worry are useless. Nor is money worth anything, for its own sake. Quality of life is what counts. Of course, such truisms are well known, but it is interesting how such things can be accepted and forgotten all in one breath!

■ WISDOM

Capricorn wisdom often appears most potently with age – indeed, the 'Wise Crone' or 'Wise Old Man' are Capricornian archetypes. Sometimes Capricorn may look back and see things could have been easier and, in fact, there were less difficult paths that would have led to the same achievement. Capricorn tends to gain in facts and experience, rather than in theories. There may be a profound acceptance and identification with Nature. The ancients called the sign of Capricorn the Gate of Souls, and indeed there is a mystery to this sign. Sometimes the true mastery of the body and the material world attained by Capricorn has its own way of opening the doors of holistic perception – a great gift to and from the Earth sign.

■ PRACTICE AND CHANGE ■

Health

- Perhaps the best 'tonic' for your health could be the deep realisation that overwork is bad for you, and that if it continues there is a substantial risk that you will not be able to work at all. It is your duty to take relaxation as well as to do your tasks.

- Remember the power of smiling. By a system of biofeedback, if you smile often enough your brain will get the message that you are happy – and happiness is good for you! Of course, when you are really feeling down, it is foolish and empty to grin, and at such times your unhappiness needs to be taken seriously. However, for the ordinary glooms and 'Monday blues' a smile can do wonders – and it is so good when people smile back!

- If you are ill or depressed, seek help sooner rather than later. There are no prizes for stoicism.

- Be prepared to make radical and creative changes in your attitude and lifestyle, where appropriate.

- Remember, enjoyment is good for you.

Wealth

- If you are a 'Scrooge' is this making you happy, or are you really living on fear? Isn't it time you bought yourself some luxuries? You can't take it with you!

- If you are the type of Capricorn who is 'managing and worrying' maybe you are addicted to hardship. There could be ways of setting yourself free that you have not considered, because deep inside you are convinced it can't be any better. It can. Get yourself some debt counselling – yes, there may be people who know how to do this better than you! – and be prepared to make some radical changes.

7

Style and leisure

Absence of occupation is not rest,
A mind quite vacant is a mind distressed

William Cowper, *Retirement*

■ YOUR LEISURE

'Capricorn leisure' is almost a contradiction in terms! Of course, there are lazy Goats among you, but it is more characteristic of this sign to feel deeply uneasy if you are not suitably employed. As we have seen, many Capricorns are so involved with their work that they have little time to play. Furthermore, you may feel uneasy at having nothing that you 'should' do. Enjoying yourself may be the most onerous and puzzling task of all!

Of course, it is not healthy to be working all the time and we are all aware that we should take regular breaks for our own good. However, to insist that you take time off to lounge around may be to condemn you to agonising discomfort that isn't at all good for you in any way. The Goat is usually happier if some form of task, duty or purpose is assigned. It is possible that certain Capricorns can make almost a duty out of watching every television programme going, and somewhere inside this square-eyed Goat probably does feel a compulsion not to miss anything. In addition, a depressed Capricorn, or one who has not yet found that focus in life, can give a good impression of fecklessness and idleness. However, you are usually much better at enjoying yourselves if you have an objective in mind.

For this reason productive pastimes may appeal, and you may enjoy assuming the burden of organising outings – after all, it gives you something to complain about! Sports and walks may be undertaken for the purpose of keeping the body healthy. Parties may be attended or given in order to promote the social life. Best of all, many sports and pastimes are specifically organised as part of the working life. Capricorns will happily play squash or golf with important clients or dress to kill for the company ball.

This is a sign that likes to win, and there are plenty of Capricorns who enjoy competitive sports. Capricorns may also relish the captaincy of a team. Many Capricorns are creative and may be good at 'hands on' artistic forms, such as sculpture and painting – equally some are gifted musically. Whatever you do is usually done well and thoroughly. Some representatives of the sign engage in long and painstaking research or develop a skill by endless practice. Even pleasure is taken seriously, and people who are close to Capricorns need to remember that Capricorn is sometimes happy being miserable! And then of course, there are those times when the Goat finds that fantastic, crazy side – and they are worth waiting for.

Holidays

Again, holidays are not usually the favourite Capricorn time, for they involve leaving work behind. Many Capricorns work themselves into the ground preparing for a holiday, so it is hardly worth the trouble. Others contrive to take their work with them, either literally, in books, files and lap-top or simply with the mobile phone 'so the office can get hold of me'. You can also turn holiday preparations into a considerable task, making sure you have all necessary documents in triplicate. You like to keep control when you go away, and the further and more exotic the location the more ferocious the control may be. However, the more relaxed Capricorns will relish the opportunity for reorientation provided by a break, and will find it therapeutic to 'earth' themselves, notice the world around them and be freed from schedules. They can even become quite 'scatty' as they shed day-to-day responsibilities and leave arrangements to other people. Even so, holidays may be peppered with tasks, even if this amounts to a list of places to see. Capricorns may prefer an active holiday, such as pony-trekking, and some delight in the back-to-nature of camping. Many Capricorns like history, and will be interested in anything from ancient monuments to ancient traction engines.

◼ YOUR STYLE

Capricorn style has several strands. In general this is a conventional, understated sign, preferring the subdued, the solid and traditional. Your tastes can turn to the minimalist, bare to the point of sterility and obsessively tidy. Here the 'controlled' version of Capricorn is in evidence. Also, as we have seen, Capricorn can be zany, and there are Goats who favour the whimsical and bohemian. In addition there are Capricorns who are cluttered and chaotic. This may be hard to understand, but the underlying dynamic is still one of 'control' – and utilitarianism. Capricorn is a very utilitarian sign, and the function of objects may be much more important than their visual appeal. Thus, you may tolerate a heap of 'useful' objects 'because they will come in handy' and Capricorn homes may be full of coat hangers, carrier bags and empty cartons.

However, the emphasis on usefulness can become an obsession to find a use for anything, ending in the Capricorn being owned by her or his possessions – not the other way round! Nonetheless, there is generally an underlying order in Capricornian lifestyle, and what may appear an utter mess to anyone else to Capricorn means control of the environment and organisation!

Capricorns often like traditional furniture in solid wood, rich and serviceable fabrics and generally objects that 'do their job'. There is rarely a place for something that is merely pretty. Pictures of natural scenes may be preferred. Old favourites may be adhered to, such as a coffee mug that is just the right size and is stained through the glaze from years of loving use, or perhaps a special spoon, pen or pair of scissors. Capricorns often have a few family hand-me-downs in pride of place, and, like Cancer, there is often a collection of some sort – CDs, books, golfing trophies – gathering dust somewhere.

Capricorns like their clothes to create a good impression and will choose for quality and cut. This sign is capable of extremely tasteful and elegant dressing, often the knack of appearing well-to-do even when on their uppers. Not for you the shoddy and down-at-heel! Usually the style is sober and clothes are chosen to 'do the job' although there are plenty of Giddy Goats who dress in ethnic fashion or sport outlandish ties.

When you are choosing purchases for yourself or your home, think useful, sensible, elegant, traditional, durable, creative, natural, solid, good quality.

You may hesitate before buying, but remember, however hard you think about it mistakes are inevitable at times!

■ PRACTICE AND CHANGE ■

- Don't be forced to take time off with nothing to do – there should always be scope for you to feel useful. However, it will do you Capricorns good to remind yourselves to lighten up a little, from time to time.

- Leisure activities should have an objective and sometimes a challenge.

- Pastimes should be absorbing. A creative hobby with an 'end product' may be very satisfying, such as building or making something.

- Holidays should generally be fairly active and structured – preferably by you.

- Your environment should be useful, and should serve you. You may need a reminder that things are there for your needs – you are not there in order to use the things.

- Your surroundings should be traditional, serviceable and comfortable. This Earth sign appreciates physical comfort.

- Your home should include an area where work brought home can be done conveniently.

- You like to create a good impression in choice of clothes. For this to be effective, you do need to take fashion into consideration. Capricorn is sometimes old-fashioned, but there is no point in buying an excellent pair of trousers if they are several centimetres too short.

- There really is no point in hanging on to old clothes because they still have life in them, unless you are one of those creative Capricorns who is going to alter them. In letting go of old clothes you are not letting go of your past and all that you hold dear, you are just getting rid of – old clothes.

Appendix 1

■ CAPRICORN COMBINED WITH MOON SIGN

Our 'birth sign' or 'star sign' refers to the sign of the zodiac occupied by the Sun when we were born. This is also called our 'Sun sign' and this book is concerned with Capricorn as a Sun sign. However, as we saw in the Introduction, a horoscope means much more than the position of the Sun alone. All the other planets have to be taken into consideration by an astrologer. Of great importance is the position of the Moon.

The Moon completes a tour of the zodiac in about twenty-eight days, changing sign every two days or so. The Moon relates to our instincts, responses, reactions, habits, comfort zone and 'where we live' emotionally – and sometimes physically. It is very important in respect of our intuitional abilities and our capacity to feel part of our environment, but because what the Moon rules is usually non-verbal and non-rational; it has been neglected. This has meant that our lives have become lop-sided. Learning to be friends with our instincts can lead to greater well-being and wholeness.

Consult the table on page 79 to find which sign the Moon was in, at the time of your birth. This, combined with your Sun sign is a valuable clue to deeper understanding.

Find your Moon number

Look up your month and day of birth. Then read across to find your personal Moon number. Now go to Chart 2, below.

January		February		March		April		May		June	
1,2	1	1,2	3	1,2	3	1,2	5	1,2	6	1,2	8
3,4	2	3,4	4	3,4	4	3,4	6	3,4	7	3,4	9
5,6	3	5,6	5	5,6	5	5,6	7	5,6	8	5,6,7	10
7,8	4	7,8	6	7,8	6	7,8	8	7,8	9	8,9	11
9,10	5	9,10,11	7	9,10	7	9,10,11	9	9,10	10	10,11,12	12
11,12	6	12,13	8	11,12	8	12,13	10	11,12,13	11	13,14	1
13,14	7	14,15	9	13,14	9	14,15,16	11	14,15,16	12	15,16,17	2
15,16,17	8	16,17,18	10	15,16,17	10	17,18	12	17,18	1	18,19	3
18,19	9	19,20	11	18,19	11	19,20,21	1	19,20	2	20,21	4
20,21	10	21,22,23	12	20,21,22	12	22,23	2	21,22,23	3	22,23	5
22,23,24	11	24,25	1	23,24,25	1	24,25	3	24,25	4	24,25	6
25,26	12	26,27,28	2	26,27	2	26,27,28	4	26,27	5	26,27	7
27,28,29	1	29	3	28,29	3	29,30	5	28,29	6	28,29,30	8
30,31	2			30,31	4			30,31	7		

July		August		September		October		November		December	
1,2	9	1	10	1,2	12	1,2	1	1,2,3	3	1,2	4
3,4	10	2,3	11	3,4	1	3,4	2	4,5	4	3,4	5
5,6,7	11	4,5,6	12	5,6,7	2	5,6	3	6,7	5	5,6	6
8,9	12	7,8	1	8,9	3	7,8,9	4	8,9	6	7,8,9	7
10,11,12	1	9,10	2	10,11	4	10,11	5	10,11	7	10,11	8
13,14	2	11,12,13	3	12,13	5	12,13	6	12,13	8	12,13	9
15,16	3	14,15	4	14,15	6	14,15	7	14,15	9	14,15	10
17,18	4	16,17	5	16,17	7	16,17	8	16,17,18	10	16,17	11
19,20	5	18,19	6	18,19	8	18,19	9	19,20	11	18,19,20	12
21,22,23	6	20,21	7	20,21,22	9	20,21	10	21,22,23	12	21,22	1
24,25	7	22,23	8	23,24	10	22,23,24	11	24,25	1	23,24,25	2
26,27	8	24,25	9	25,26,27	11	25,26	12	26,27,28	2	26,27	3
28,29	9	26,27,28	10	28,29	12	27,28,29	1	29,30	3	28,29	4
30,31	10	29,30	11	30	1	30,31	2			30,31	5
		31	12								

Find your Moon sign

Find your year of birth. Then read across to the column of your Moon number. Where they intersect shows your Moon sign.

Birth year					Moon number										
					1	2	3	4	5	6	7	8	9	10	11	12
1900	1919	1938	1957	1976												
1901	1920	1939	1958	1977												
1902	1921	1940	1959	1978												
1903	1922	1941	1960	1979												
1904	1923	1942	1961	1980												
1905	1924	1943	1962	1981												
1906	1925	1944	1963	1982												
1907	1926	1945	1964	1983												
1908	1927	1946	1965	1984												
1909	1928	1947	1966	1985												
1910	1929	1948	1967	1986												
1911	1930	1949	1968	1987												
1912	1931	1950	1969	1988												
1913	1932	1951	1970	1989												
1914	1933	1952	1971	1990												
1915	1934	1953	1972	1991												
1916	1935	1954	1973	1992												
1917	1936	1955	1974	1993												
1918	1937	1956	1975	1994												

Ari   Tau   Gem   Can   Leo   Vir   Lib   Sco   Sag   Cap   Aqu   Pis

Capricorn Sun / Capricorn Moon

Caution rules, OK? You possess the inner conviction that the world is a conspiracy to catch you with your pants down. As you are quite determined that this will not happen, life becomes uncomfortable at times. You are a definite control freak, determined not to show your feelings and to keep tabs on all your surroundings. You are always happier when you have found the drawback in any situation, for then you know you can cope – it is the unknown that fazes you. Suspicious? – yes, at times. However, you are a supremely capable soul and people know they can rely on you utterly. You have a whimsical streak, an unexpected wit, and you can be an innovator, in your chosen field (as long as this does not involve too many risks). When you give your heart it is probably forever. Remember to let others give to you as well as giving yourself, and that if you do not state your needs they cannot possibly be met by others. And ask yourself whether the standards you follow are *really* valid, for you. If not, move on.

Capricorn Sun / Aquarius Moon

Intimacy is not easy for you, and you may respond to it by distancing yourself, or by trying to control the situation. You prefer to rely on yourself and, deep down, you rarely trust others to provide the support you need. Perhaps you prefer to be committed to your work, and this may be a defence against relating. Your reactions sometimes surprise you and you would secretly like to be more unpredictable and unconventional than you allow – however, others notice that you can be erratic and you may take out your need for freedom on your nearest and dearest, by denying them close access. You can be an inspired and creative thinker, and you should follow your hunches a little more. You have both practicality and originality. Remind yourself that true freedom comes from acknowledging and meeting feelings and needs, not by denying them.

Capricorn Sun / Pisces Moon

You conceal your tender heart very well, but those close to you know that your bark is worse than your bite. Probably you avoid situations where your innate caution may be subverted by a rush of feeling, but deep inside your emotions are powerful. Often strict about routine and responsibility, an escapist streak sometimes emerges in you. You are dynamic and achieve a great deal, especially when this concerns helping others, and you have the gratifying talent of being able to make real your dreams. Both practical and intuitive, you are most astute about the human race and you prefer to help those who are prepared to help themselves. But who rescues the rescuer? In between being sensible and circumspect, and on the other hand losing yourself in others, you may lose sight of what is really you, and what you need. Open your heart to the love of your own 'inner child' and take care of yourself, also.

Capricorn Sun / Aries Moon

It is possible that you spend considerable time kicking yourself – and possibly the cat! Be careful that you do not take out your frustrations on others or expect them to provide for you what you must give yourself – self-validation. You may deny your need for closeness, while being unconsciously demanding, and even impossible at times! You may find you lose your temper, or that sudden impulsiveness destroys all your painstaking plans. Despite your practicality, there is a part of you, deep inside, that does not always feel 'real'. You are a tremendously dynamic person, with the common sense to create much that is valuable, enduring and imaginative, too. What you need to work at is getting the balance right. 'Render unto Caesar that which is Caesar's' by accepting limitations, where necessary and by not expecting others to pander to your whims – but let your soul go soaring to empower your physical endeavours. If you are not a high achiever, you ought to be!

Capricorn Sun / Taurus Moon

You are a very stable and pragmatic soul. It is important to you to be able to rely on yourself and you place a priority on providing security and comfort. Practical to a high degree, you may over-emphasise the need for money, sex and materialistic reward – 'hyacinths for the soul' may have little meaning for you and, in fact, you may scorn all such. Although you like routine, and you tend to hang on to things and people well past sell-by date, you are also able to enjoy yourself, and life often seems to run smoothly for you – to observers, at least! You probably have many tangible and rewarding achievements to your credit. Deep inside you may doubt your self-sufficiency and defend constantly against the horror of having unmet needs by being relentlessly self-sufficient and planning. Guard against patterns of laziness and make room in your life for imagination. Ask yourself what your real needs may be and whether there is really more to life than sex, food, a nice home and money in the bank. There is! And if you have trust enough in the universe to appreciate this you will discover a deep trust in yourself that will wipe away any insecurity.

Capricorn Sun / Gemini Moon

You may feel that your environment is unstable, or uncertain, and compensate for this by being prepared for everything – something of a strain, that may make you nervy at times, but resourceful. Although you may be quite chatty and gregarious, it is not easy to get close to you. You are curious and interested in many subjects, so while you may choose a 'steady' lifestyle, your need for variety and stimulation must also be catered for, and you may surprise people by your quick thought or by a habit of taking off on journeys or changing plans at the last minute. Being a swift, empiric thinker, your ideas probably have class and versatility as well as being sound and useful. You like challenge and stimulation, up to a point, and you have a hunger for knowledge. However, your talents are wasted when they are used to reason away your own needs. Emotions are a difficult area for you. If a feeling gets as far as even being acknowledged it then gets stamped out by 'realism' or relegated to a practical requirement. Stop rationalising, and try to communicate your true needs, so you can achieve rapport as well as factual communication and 'chat'.

Capricorn Sun / Cancer Moon

You have a strong need to nurture and be nurtured, and you possess the sensitivity and the common sense to achieve both. Although you can be deeply empathic, you like also to retain a sense of perspective and distance. You can be intuitive and you may have revealing dreams – certainly you should take note of your dreams. You may be afraid of 'letting go' which means that although you can be kind and responsive, at a deep level you hold back. Because you are so sensitive you may have developed resourceful ways of coping with things that serve rather to keep needs in check than to satisfy them. Home is probably important to you, and you may be possessive. You need to give as much place in your life to the soundless pull of instinct as you do to the 'useful' – then you can come up with ideas that are really inspired. Rest assured that if you communicate your real needs, you will not be overwhelmed, and neither will anyone else. Build sufficient inner security so that you do not find closeness threatening.

Capricorn Sun / Leo Moon

Sometimes you are an embarrassment to yourself, for while you are doing your best to be calm, cool and collected, somehow you find yourself coming on like the lead in the fifth-form drama or making a necklace of paper clips when you should be working. At others you succeed in maintaining an urbane exterior that serves your purpose, which is likely to be self-advancement of some kind. You are very ambitious, and you nurture large-scale plans and flamboyant dreams. Fortunately for you, you have the nuts and bolts to put it all together, and you should go far. A warm-hearted person, you like to have some 'standing' – you are a mixture of magnanimity and self-importance. You can be charitable and generous, but you like to be thanked! Do not try to repress your desire for attention, for you need to bask in the warmth of acclaim, in order to function creatively and to give of yourself. Don't be too stern with the child within – give it love and appreciation, temper its urges with common sense and channel its imagination.

Capricorn Sun / Virgo Moon

You may meet yourself coming backwards, so concerned are you to be prepared for all eventualities, cope with every detail and do things perfectly. Yes, for the most part you function more than admirably, and others may be staggered by your efficiency – you are rarely 'caught on the hop' and may regularly achieve excellent results. I hesitate to give you anything but praise, for all else you are likely to take as criticism! In general it would be better to try to live life instead of analysing it, and, yes, to stop being your own most avid critic. You may adopt routines that function perfectly but remain somewhat narrow. It is hard to imagine a more capable person, but even your capability could be enhanced by the relaxation that comes from tolerance of your own imperfections. Your universe will not disassemble if you allow all your feelings into consciousness, for then you will be able to sort and prioritise them. Whose standards are these anyhow? Develop the self-love and acceptance to form your own yardsticks.

Capricorn Sun / Libra Moon

Your sense of aesthetics is probably refined, and no doubt you have principles and ideals in regard to relationships. You may indeed be quite artistic. It is important to you to form close bonds, but your reserve and idealism may make rapport elusive. Rather than face anything discordant, you will withdraw – but being a 'good' partner may mean showing anger at times, so the relationship can have vitality rather than remain a courtly dance. You can be objective, and are able to weigh things up before taking efficient action. You may be a skilful and subtle tactician, with a talent for getting the best out of people and achieving your ends, while convincing others it is what they want, or even thought of in the first place. You may be annoyed and unsettled at your own indecisiveness and may choose to get on with practicalities, where you can achieve some-thing, cutting off your emotional side – or you may exert yourself being useful and pleasing to others, while being stern about your own needs. In this you are denying other people the gratification of fulfilling you, and they may experience this as witholding. Listen to all the voices within you: you have a right to express yourself, to find the inner peace that comes from acceptance (not repression) and to surround yourself with beauty.

Capricorn Sun / Scorpio Moon

You are a private person, and while you may find sensible ways to cope with your intense emotions, you are still concerned with keeping control. If your true needs are not met, you may turn to sexual gratification or excessive preoccupation with money. You are probably interested in the hidden, in some respect, and may be a sleuth, drawn to the occult, or simply have a nose for good deals, other people's motives and feelings or the inner workings of the world in general. You are a force to be reckoned with if you bear grudges – which you may. However, gratification will come to you only by drawing on your inner power and depths and facing and meeting your own needs, rather than manipulating or punishing others. Capable of empathy and profound understanding, you can put your soul into what you do and achieve the unforgettable – in business, art, homemaking and a variety of spheres. Accept all your feelings, not just the sexual ones. That is real 'self-possession'.

Capricorn Sun / Sagittarius Moon

Which does your restrained exterior conceal? The clown, the philosopher, or the playful child? The answer is doubtless all three, and more besides. As you plod steadily ahead those itchy feet may long to break into a dance. You have access to a huge variety of ideas and inspirations and it is likely that your aspirations are sky-high. Because you insist on the practical, yours are not just pipe-dreams and you may be one of life's high-fliers – however, you may still be discontented. In an effort to bring a sense of meaning into your life you may adopt a severe or demanding moral code, but that is not the path to enlightenment. Combine your talent for mastery with your brilliant imagination, to create something unique. Seek neither to crystallise the spiritual and inspirational, nor to dodge method and experience. Inner freedom comes from working – gladly – within limitations, and you are capable of bringing a sparkle to the mundane. Human closeness, too, is important, so don't philosophise yourself out of your needs or attend, emptily, to duty. Openness and vibrant emotion can also be paths to inspiration.

Appendix 2

■ ZODIACAL COMPATIBILITY

To assess fully the compatibility of two people the astrologer needs to have the entire chart of each individual, and while Sun-sign factors will be noticeable, there is a legion of other important points to be taken into account. Venus and Mercury are always very close to the Sun, and while these are often in the Sun sign itself, so intensifying its effect, they may also fall in one of the signs lying on either side of your Sun sign. So, as a 'Capricorn' you may have Venus and/or Mercury in Aquarius or Sagittarius, and this will increase your empathy with these signs. In addition, the Moon and all the other planets including the Ascendant and Midheaven need to be taken into account. So if you have always been drawn to Gemini people, perhaps you have Moon or Ascendant in Gemini.

In order to give a vivid character sketch, things have to be stated graphically. You should look for the dynamics at work, rather than be too literal about interpretation – for instance, you may find that you do not argue too much with Aries people, but you are aware that there is tension and contrast. It is up to the two of you whether a relationship works, for it can, if you are both committed. Part of achieving that is using the awareness you have to help, not necessarily as a reason for abandoning the relationship. There are always points of compatibility and we are here to learn from each other.

On a scale of 1 (worst) to 4 (best), here is a table to assess instantly the superficial compatibility rating between Capricorn and companions:

Capricorn 3	Cancer 3
Aquarius 1	Leo 2
Pisces 4	Virgo 4
Aries 2	Libra 2
Taurus 4	Scorpio 3
Gemini 1	Sagittarius 2

■ CAPRICORN COMPATIBILITIES

Capricorn with Capricorn

You are both hard working and ambitious, and it is probable that you can achieve a comfortable lifestyle together. Each of you likes to be in control, but as long as there is agreement about who does what there should never be an argument about who takes out the dustbins! Both pragmatic and down-to-earth, your household should run like clockwork (unless one or both of you has lots of planets in Fire or Water). If you decide to have a family it is quite likely that 2.4 children will arrive on schedule, like most other things in life. As you both put duty before pleasure, there is a chance that all work and no play could make this a dull, if enduring marriage. You must take time out for each other, for simple play and spontaneity.

As lovers   The sex life of two Earth signs is often healthy and regular, if a little lacking in electricity. Ms Capricorn realises that this is a man she can rely on. Mr Capricorn feels that this is a woman who will enhance, not threaten, his stability. You may both be career orientated and one obstacle could be if you each have high-powered jobs that take you to opposite ends of the country. There may be a feeling of 'you and me against the world' as each of you struggles against the inevitable burdens that find Capricorns (or is it the other way round...?). Alternatively you may lock horns with each other over details – and, if so, you must ask yourselves if these really matter. Capricorn is a hierarchical sign and it shouldn't be too difficult to decide who runs what – neither can run everything. Closeness, trust, shared responsibilities and possessions all add up to make this a very durable partnership indeed.

As friends   Lots in common, your friendship can endure through long separation and distance, for neither makes friends easily. Shared interests in planning, business, crafts, history.

As business partners   Sound and driving onwards. You should go far, but not in meteoric style.

Capricorn with Aquarius

Some Aquarians are fairly 'saturnine', and with these more stable types certain factors resemble the Capricorn/Capricorn couple. However, with the more zany Aquarians there may be little point of contact. Capricorn will find Aquarius interesting, but is unlikely to attempt a close relationship if Aquarius is too freedom orientated. Intellectual partnership may be stimulating, but emotion could be conspicuous by its absence.

As lovers   At first sex could be exciting. However, Aquarian tendency to detachment and Capricorn prioritising of duty could mean that sex falls by the wayside and no one bothers. However, in the long run Aquarius can become bored and Capricorn needful of closer contact. Ms Capricorn may admire the coolness of this man and the way he retains the courage of his convictions, however off-beat his views, while Mr Capricorn is intrigued by the independence and unpredictability of Ms Aquarius. However, unless there are close contacts between other planets the emotional voltage is likely to be low, and this couple may live independent lifestyles. Of course, this suits some.

As friends   The Aquarian preoccupation with 'Universal truth' may sit awkwardly with Capricornian pragmatism, and Aquarius may feel Capricorn is narrow and selfish, while Capricorn feels Aquarius is unstable. However, some Capricorns develop a reserved idealism, realising that their search for mastery is incomplete without deeper awareness. In this case there can be much discussion, with Aquarius giving interesting perspectives and Capricorn introducing common sense. At a more mundane level, both signs can be practical and may make plans together.

As business partners   Can work well as long as Aquarius has some good ideas and isn't too erratic. Aquarian lack of ambition may irritate Capricorn, and Aquarius may say Capricorn is too profit orientated – and what about the environment, the jobless, etc.

Capricorn with Pisces

This can be an excellent partnership, for Capricorn provides the security and stability needed in the Watery world of the Mer-person, while Pisces rolls away the stone, encouraging Capricorn to loosen up and dream, without presenting too much conflict. Trouble may arise if Capricorn crushes Piscean dreams or is generally insensitive, while Pisces can make a hopeless muddle out of Capricorn's tidy world and drive her or him hairless.

As lovers   Sex can be blissful, for Piscean responsiveness is gratifying and heart warming to Capricorn, while Pisces feels safe to be vulnerable with the Goat. There is an old-fashioned romanticism and a soft heart in many Capricorns, which Pisces unerringly reveals, while Pisces is often given a sound basis on which to build his or her artistic endeavours. Ms Capricorn delights in this gentle, whimsical man, while Mr Capricorn finds Ms Pisces magical, and all his protective instincts are aroused. Capricorn's leadership is not challenged by Pisces – the only problem may be that Pisces forgets to follow! Providing Capricorn is able to be gentle with Pisces, and Pisces to appreciate that Capricorn isn't being boring but has the capability to flesh out some of the dreams, this partnership can work very well.

As friends   Pisces can stimulate the fantasy side of Capricorn, and there may be some intriguing adventures, while Capricorn provides Pisces with some organisation. However, there are times when Capricorn can be crushingly prosaic and Pisces too flimsy to be true, and then the common ground becomes a deserted beach.

As business partners   Capricorn is not a confident sign and Pisces may do little to offset this, for Piscean wild ideas bring the Goat out in goosebumps. The result may be that nothing gets off the ground. However, where Capricorn is sure footed, Pisces can show new vistas.

Capricorn with Aries

There is often a strong attraction here – usually one of opposites. Aries lives for today and lets tomorrow take care of itself, while Capricorn takes care of everything. These signs share an ambitious streak, and both are quite convinced they know the best way forward – in opposite directions. However, if they can get their horses to pull together, this is a chariot that heads for the land of dreams – by a bumpy, circuitous route!

As lovers   Sexual attraction may be very strong, as is often the case between Fire and Earth signs. Ms Capricorn is bowled over by the assertiveness of Mr Aries (although you'd never guess!) and

Mr Capricorn finds Ms Aries exciting and challenging. There is something about the way that Aries cuts through red tape that appeals to Capricorn – although, of course, it depends whose red tape! Aries has an 'always right' streak, which brings out the same in Capricorn, and care needs to be taken that domestic life doesn't degenerate to squabbles about where to keep the sugar bowl.

As friends   Capricorn finds Aries inspiring and enjoys putting into practice all the viable schemes – Aries does cheer the Goat out of some of the worse chasms of despair. Sometimes Capricorn finds Aries too pushy, and then the hooves go in and Capricorn can be neither pushed nor led – at such moments each may feel at the limit of frustration. But mostly you have much to offer each other.

As business partners   This may be dynamic and effectual. Aries will want to be boss, but it is better that Capricorn should steer the ship, guiding Arien flamboyant ideas around financial rocks.

Capricorn with Taurus

These two Earth signs can make an excellent and enduring partnership, for they talk the same pragmatic language. Both prioritise security and financial solvency. Taurus is able to bring a Venusian measure of peace and beauty into the life of the Goat – but rarely poetry. There may be a lack of a certain something, that neither can put their practical finger on, and the relationship may be an enduring one with both partners telling themselves sternly that romance is not important. Maybe not, but . . . .

As lovers   Taurus is the most sensuous sign of the zodiac and this is answered by the restrained lustiness of Capricorn, so sex may be excellent, if lacking a certain magic at times. Ms Capricorn feels very safe with Taurus, who is often an excellent earner, while

Mr Capricorn feels this is a woman who has her priorities right. Both of these signs can be stubborn, however, and while Capricorn is often open to being convinced, Taurus doesn't always bother with logic and may simply obstruct – or worse still, issue abrupt commands. Then we have the recipe for a rock-like impasse. It is best if each partner has her or his own area of control, which might have worked fine in the old days, when the woman minded house while the man went out to work. Today more effort may be needed to establish boundaries, and respect them.

As friends   Misunderstandings are unlikely, and these two can be very close and comfortable together, offering mutual – and often practical – support. Enjoyment of similar things can ensure some happy excursions.

As business partners   No fireworks here, but the prospect of steady growth. Capricorn may find Taurean lack of ambition a trifle galling at times.

Capricorn with Gemini

The Geminian liveliness may be dubbed 'flighty' by Capricorn and each may bring out the worst in each other, Capricorn going to repressive extremes while Gemini elevates inconsistency to an art. However, there may be an attraction here, for Capricorn may spot the usefulness of some of Gemini's ideas, admiring the versatility and communicative ability of the sign.

As lovers   Sex life may be inventive at first. However, Gemini is usually too detached and unpredictable to answer Capricorn's need for solid contact and gratification. Ms Capricorn is often fascinated by this brilliant and charming character, while Mr Capricorn's macho instincts may be aroused by flirty Ms Gemini. However,

Gemini may find Capricorn depressing after a while and Capricorn may become unhappy and possessive – or plain frustrated. Capricorn may decide to detach from the partnership rather than to take risks with emotions or finances. However, with effort this can work for Gemini can benefit from the stability offered and Capricorn can find life more amusing with Geminian sparkle. Also Capricorn is not over-prone to emotionality, so problems can be reasoned out.

As friends   There may be some fun in planning things together, but Capricorn may feel that Gemini is too easily distracted from the important factors – which Gemini finds boring. Emotional rapport is not likely to be strong, but if there is common intellectual ground you can show each other some differing perspectives.

As business partners   This can be the best sort of contact, providing there is scope for Geminian resourcefulness and inventiveness. Capricorn should do the organising, while Gemini deals with promotions.

Capricorn with Cancer

These may each admire what they see reflected in their zodiacal opposite. Capricornian stability is a tonic to Cancer, while the Crab's tenacity answers something within Capricorn. These two may feather their nest together until old age. However, Cancer can be very touchy. When the emotional storms roll in, Capricorn just plods doggedly onwards, whereas Cancer may feel very upset and dub the Goat 'insensitive'. Neither of these two knows when to give up on a bad job and an unsatisfactory marriage may endure, to the depression of mutual friends, as well as the couple concerned.

As lovers   The sexual side of the relationship can be tender and loving. Cancer's high sex-drive and emotional richness can bring out the best in Capricorn, and if the Goat does put business before pleasure Cancer will understand this if it is the home that is being worked for. Ms Cancer is drawn to the providence that Mr Capricorn wears like a badge, while Mr Capricorn is attracted by the sheer 'old-fashioned feminity' that many Cancerian females exude. Here we have a conservative couple, for the most part. Capricorn is a dynastic sign and Cancer often loves to have children, so there may be a large family to carry on 'the name' and receive the legacy of combined thrift.

As friends There is much to recommend this friendship, for Capricorn is less likely to upset Cancer where the emotional expectations are less intense. Cancer can add warmth to Capricorn, while Capricorn offers the supportive friendship the Crab needs.

As business partners Rather an overcautious duo, but Cancer can supply the imaginative and creative stimulus. You are both ambitious and active, and with Capricorn's strategic talents you could go far, at a stately pace.

Capricorn with Leo

Often Capricorn is really going where Leo likes to appear to be, thus the Lion may love Capricornian ambition and achievement, while Capricorn sees in Leo the repressed flames within his or her own soul. However, this promising start may founder when Capricorn becomes as repressive and punitive with Leo as the Goat is with his or her own 'inner child', and Leo becomes outraged. If you can remember what first attracted you and continue to admire the ambition within the other, then this partnership stands a better chance.

As lovers As with many Fire/Earth attractions, this can get off to a noisy start. Leo certainly can ignite Capricorn, while the Goat has a reassuring effect on Leo. Ms Capricorn recognises the playful boy in dramatic Mr Leo and may feel strangely protective and magnetised. Mr Capricorn, with that unerring eye, recognises that this flamboyant lady is just the sort to have on his arm. However, each wants to be boss, and Capricorn can get resentful tidying up after Leo and of Leo accusing Capricorn of being a stick-in-the-mud. Pride can give rise to a granite-hard impasse. Remember the crackle of that early chemistry, and how you said 'Vive la difference'. Your relationship can work, but a little humility and lots of adaptability need to be fostered.

As friends Without sexual attraction there may be little to bring these two together, and if companionship develops each of you is likely to want to run the show. However, where friendship is established, respect and loyalty can run very deep.

As business partners Possibly excellent. Capricorn must manage the money and do the planning. Promotions and big ideas are Leo's department. Again, respect is essential.

Capricorn with Virgo

These two Earth signs have a great deal in common. Capricorn respects the Virgoan eye for detail. However, you may meet each other coming backwards striving to be prepared for everything and have more passion for excellence than each other. Nonetheless, you talk the same language and will each feel secure in the pragmatism of the other.

As lovers Sex is likely to go smoothly, although perhaps with a meat-and-two-veg quality. This duo can work excellently, but you need to be careful you do not become obsessed with pruning hedges and picking nits – and entirely missing the shower of shooting stars.

Who needs a shooting star? *You do* – to wish on, and make sure you wish for a little of the celestial to enhance your relationship. Ms Capricorn is impressed by the quiet capability of Mr Virgo, and Mr Capricorn loves this woman's elegance and subtle sex appeal. Don't get side-tracked into trivia – regularly review goals and keep the sensual side of your relationship well fed. As Earth signs you know so well how to do this, but you may not always bother.

As friends You can support each other through moods of anxiety and times of stress. Virgo should not become a servant for Capricorn. You can plan excursions with military precision and it may be important for you to share activities rather than sitting around. Capricorn is less communicative than Virgo and may need to work at this.

As business partners The danger is that you will disappear inside yourselves, dotting i's and crossing t's and never sending the contracts off. On the other hand, if you really get going yours is a precision vehicle that is not headed for the stars but to well-insured prosperity.

Capricorn with Libra

There is much to attract these two, for the Libran refinement and stylishness appeals to Capricorn's sense of the socially advantageous – and, let's face it, to their dormant aesthetic sensibilities. Capricorn is decisive and can give lazy Libra a gentle kick in the posterior to make the best of talents possessed. However, Capricorn may feel strained by Libra's social instincts – 'Oh, we're not having company *again*, are we'? and Libra can find Capricorn a killjoy.

As lovers These two may have a good sexual relationship, as long as Capricorn learns a few courtly graces. This is very important for the warmth of the relationship. Ms Capricorn finds Mr Libra very polished and admires his urbanity, while Mr Capricorn is charmed by stylish Libra. The trouble may be that Capricorn may see no need at all to talk about the relationship – doing is more their style – and Libra, despite the Earthy presence, may feel lonely. Capricorn needs to work at communication and Libra should resort to coaxing – not nagging.

As friends   Capricorn is possibly the best sign to persuade Libra to get off his or her butt, and both may enjoy the stylish result that planning with pizzazz can achieve. However, Capricorn may find Libra lightweight and superficial. Libra can bring grace and vitality to Capricorn's social life, and as both signs can be rational there may be points of contact. Libran skills appeal to Capricorn's instinct for social climbing. Capricorn just must not be a wet blanket.

As business partners   Libra is more dash than cash, and while Capricorn may admire that polished image, improvidence will cause them sleepless nights. Capricorn must be the money-bags, but must listen well to Libran calls for style.

Capricorn with Scorpio

This is a heavyweight matter, of Gothic gloom or depth and commitment. Both these signs are jealous and possessive, and Capricorn is stoical in the face of Scorpionic suspicions. Laughs may be a bit thin on the ground, unless there are plenty of planets in Fire and Air signs. You could make each other depressed, or be mutually supportive. Don't take it all so *seriously*!

As lovers   These are strongly sexed signs and usually find each other profoundly satisfying. It is said that 'If sex is wrong, it's 90 per cent of a relationship, if it's right it's 10 per cent but for these two it may be 90 per cent anyway, for it is a great source of closeness and satisfaction in two very reserved signs. Ms Capricorn is drawn to the hidden depths of Scorpio, while Mr Capricorn is often fascinated by the smouldering quality of Ms Scorpio. Indestructible moods can set in with resentments maggotting away for years – quite literally. Scorpionic intensity can be beyond Capricorn, and so Scorpio may feel isolated. Capricorn may feel bewildered and insecure at emotional demands, but instead of admitting this, stony silence can rule the day. Force yourselves to talk about your feelings – this is often a long-lasting partnership and how long can you keep that lip buttoned?

As friends   Here there is often great loyalty and durability even if you are separated for long periods. Scorpio helps Capricorn to appreciate the depths and subtleties of human interaction, which the Goat doesn't always understand in all its ramifications, but may come to accept and cope with. In turn, Capricorn common sense can have a stabilising effect on Scorpio.

As business partners   You both tend to see the worms rather than the apples and may be overcautious. A Fire sign on board can add optimism and flair.

Capricorn with Sagittarius

Sagittarian joyful abandon can be a tonic to Capricorn, or leave the Goat looking like a Rottweiler chewing on a wasp. The best hope for this partnership is that each has planets in the other's sign, otherwise the differences may be too hard to surmount. Capricorn's structured life is threatened by the joyful Archer, and that perpetually unlocked back door may send the Goat into neurosis. On the plus side, Capricorn can inject some structure into the Sagittarian whirl, while Sagittarius can cheer up Capricorn. However, there is no doubt that this partnership needs lots of work.

As lovers Here we have Fire and Earth again, and attraction is often strong, especially at first. Ms Capricorn longs to be the one to bring this wild boy home, while Mr Capricorn is galvanised by Ms Sagittarius. Capricorn manages practicalities without apparent effort, and Sagittarius (who may well have a horror of the car and the cooker) can't help appreciating this. Capricorn may find the irresponsibility of Sagittarius weighs heavily for the most part, although there are times when the playful aspect of the Goat can be almost forced out by Sagittarius. Capricorn may get fed up with doing all the hard work of the relationship while Sagittarius just gets . . . fed up. However, you have much to offer each other, so try to remember that when things get fraught.

As friends Capricorn may have fun organising some of the Archer's schemes into a semblance of viability, and Sagittarius may then be able to enjoy the fruits of this. Appreciate each other!

As business partners Sagittarian initiative and sense of adventure is perfectly counter-balanced by the solidity of Capricorn – and if you can only value that fact and work with it, your enterprise will be unstoppable. Otherwise it will be unstartable.

Appendix 3

■ TRADITIONAL ASSOCIATIONS AND TOTEM

Each sign of the zodiac is said to have an affinity with certain colours, plants, stones and other substances. Of course, we cannot be definite about this, for not only do sources vary regarding specific correspondences – we also have the rest of the astrological chart to bear in mind. Some people also believe that the whole concept of such associations is invalid. However, there certainly do seem to be some links between the character of each of the signs and the properties of certain substances. It is up to you to experiment and to see what works for you.

Anything that traditionally links with Capricorn is liable to intensify Capricornian traits. So if you wish for some reason to be ebullient and unrestrained, you should steer clear of the colours dark grey and blue and of the essential oils of cypress and patchouli! Naturally, you are not restricted to oils ruled by your sign, for in many cases treatment by other oils will be beneficial, and you should consult a qualified aromatherapist for advice if you have a particular problem. However, if you want to be your Capricornian constructive best, it may help to surround yourself with the right stimuli, especially on a down day. Here are some suggestions:

- **Colours** Generally sober shades of grey, deep blue, brown and possibly black. However, Capricorns do not always like to be so downbeat and may benefit from and enjoy earthy colours in shades of greens, browns, and sometimes purple and old gold. Capricorns inspired by the 'Saturnalia' mode may choose much wilder hues.
- **Flowers** Honeysuckle, magnolia, mimosa, vervain.
- **Metal** Lead. At home, Capricorns may like solid wood, earthenware and pewter.
- **Stones** Apache tear, hematite, onyx, obsidian.

Aromatherapy

Aromatherapy uses the healing power of essential oils both to prevent ill health and to maintain good health. Specific oils can sometimes be used to treat specific ailments. Essential oils are concentrated and powerful substances and should be treated with respect. Buy from a reputable source. *Do not use any oil in pregnancy* until you have checked it is OK with a reputable source (see Further Reading). *Do not ingest oils* – they act through the subtle medium of smell, and are absorbed in massage. *Do not place undiluted on the skin.* For massage: Dilute in a carrier oil such as sweet almond or grapeseed, two drops of oil to one teaspoon of carrier. Use in an oil burner, six to ten drops at a time, to fragrance your living area.

Essential oils
- **Cypress** This earthy, woody-scented oil is said to ease grief and to promote calm in a crisis. It is good as an astringent and anti-spasmodic, for coughs, perspiration and menstruation problems.
- **Patchouli** An earthy, sensual oil, good for grounding and common sense. Has anti-inflammatory properties that help with sores, and is good for skin that is beginning to age.

- **Vetivert** Earthy and smoky, this is very relaxing and excellent for relieving stress.

Naturally you are not restricted to oils ruled by your sign, for in many cases treatment by other oils will be beneficial, and you should consult a reputable source for advice if you have a particular problem. If a problem persists, consult your GP.

Your birth totem

According to the tradition of certain native North American tribes, each of the signs of the zodiac is known by a totem animal. The idea of the totem animal is useful, for animals are powerful, living symbols and they can do much to put us in touch with our potentials. Knowing your totem animal is different from knowing your sign, for your sign is used to define and describe you – as we have been doing in this book – whereas your totem shows you a path of potential learning and growth.

The totem for Capricorn is the Goose, and you also have an affinity with Buffalo and Turtle. You were born in the Renewal Time. There is a difficulty here, for the North American lore is based on the seasonal cycle. For those of you living in the Southern Hemisphere, it is worth noting the totems of your opposite, Cancer. These are Woodpecker, also Mouse and possibly Frog of the Water clan, and the Cancerian time is called Long Days Time.

Geese often inhabit lonely and windswept moors and marshes. They were important to the Celts and have been immortalised in folk tales. They are large, determined birds and can be aggressive – they are credited with having saved Rome through their loud honking. Goose, with its power of flight, can add a new dimension to Capricornian sense of achievement, and their familiarity with deserted landscapes adds a poetry to the isolation that sometimes comes over Capricorn.

They are a symbol of the freedom and self-possession that is Capricorn's birthright.

Contacting your totem

You can use visualisation techniques to make contact with the energies of your birth totem. You will need to be very quiet, still and relaxed. Make sure you won't be disturbed. Have a picture of your totem before you and perhaps burn one of the oils we have mentioned, in an oil burner, to intensify the atmosphere. When you are ready close your eyes and imagine that you are your totem animal – imagine how it feels, what it smells, sees, hears. What are its feelings, instincts and abilities? Keep this up for as long as you are comfortable and then come back to everyday awareness. Write down your experiences and eat or drink something, to ground you. This can be a wonderfully refreshing and mind-clearing exercise, and you may find it inspiring. Naturally, if you feel you have other totem animals – creatures with which you feel an affinity – you are welcome to visualise these. Look out for your totems in the wild – there may be a message for you.

Further reading
and resources

Astrology for Lovers, Liz Greene, Unwin, 1986. The title may be misleading, for this is a serious, yet entertaining and wickedly accurate account of the signs. A table is included to help you find your Rising Sign. This book is highly recommended.

Teach Yourself Astrology, Jeff Mayo and Christine Ramsdale, Hodder & Stoughton, 1996. A classic textbook for both beginner and practising astrologer, giving a fresh insight to birth charts through a unique system of personality interpretation.

Love Signs for Beginners, Kristyna Arcarti, Hodder & Stoughton, 1995. A practical introduction to the astrology of romantic relationships, explaining the different roles played by each of the planets and focussing particularly on the position of the Moon at the time of birth.

Star Signs for Beginners, Kristyna Arcarti, Hodder & Stoughton, 1993. An analysis of each of the star signs – a handy, quick reference.

The Moon and You for Beginners, Teresa Moorey, Hodder & Stoughton, 1996. Discover how the phase of the Moon when you were born affects your personality. This book looks at the nine lunar types – how they live, love, work and play, and provides simple tables to enable you to find out your birth phase and which type you are.

The New Compleat Astrologer, Derek and Julia Parker, Mitchell Beazley, 1984. This is a complete introduction to astrology with instructions on chart calculation and planetary tables, as well as clear and interesting descriptions of planets and signs. Including history and reviewing present-day astrology, this is an extensive work, in glossy, hardback form, with colour illustrations.

The Knot of Time: Astrology and the Female Experience, Lindsay River and Sally Gillespie. For personal growth, from a gently feminine perspective, this book has much wisdom.

The Astrology of Self-discovery, Tracy Marks, CRCS Publications, 1985. This book is especially useful for Moon signs.

The Astrologer's Handbook, Francis Sakoian and Louis Acker, Penguin, 1984. This book explains chart calculation and takes the reader through the meanings of signs and planets, with extensive interpretations of planets in signs and houses. In addition, all the major aspects between planets and angles are interpreted individually. A very useful work.

Aromatherapy for Pregnancy and Childbirth, Margaret Fawcett RGN, RM, LLSA, Element, 1993.

The Aromatherapy Handbook, Daniel Ryman, C W Daniel, 1990.

Useful addresses

The Faculty of Astrological Studies
The claim of the Faculty to provide the 'finest and most comprehensive astrological tuition in the world' is well founded. Correspondence courses of a high calibre are offered, leading to the internationally recognised diploma. Evening classes, seminars and summer schools are taught, catering for the complete beginner to the most experienced astrologer. A list of trained consultants can be supplied on request, if you wish for a chart interpretation. For further details telephone (UK code) 0171 700 3556 (24-hour answering service); or fax 0171 700 6479. Alternatively, you can write, with SAE, to: Ref. T. Moorey, FAS., BM7470, London WC1N 3XX, UK.

Educational

California Institute of Integral Studies, 765 Ashbury St, San Francisco, CA 94117. Tel: (415) 753-6100

Kepler College of Astrological Arts and Sciences, 4518 University Way, NE, Suite 213, Seattle, WA 98105. Tel: (206) 633-4907

Robin Armstrong School of Astrology, Box 5265, Station 'A', Toronto, Ontario, M5W 1N5, Canada. Tel: (416) 923-7827

Vancouver Astrology School, Astraea Astrology, Suite 412, 2150 W Broadway, Vancouver, V6K 4L9, Canada. Tel: (604) 536-3880

The Southern Cross Academy of Astrology, PO Box 781147, Sandton, SA 2146 (South Africa) Tel: 11-468-1157; Fax: 11-468-1522

Periodicals

American Astrology Magazine, PO Box 140713, Staten Island, NY 10314-0713. e-mail: am.astrology@genie.gies,com

The Journal of the Seasons, PO Box 5266, Wellesley St, Auckland 1, New Zealand. Tel/fax: (0)9-410-8416

The Federation of Australian Astrologers Bulletin, PO Box 159, Stepney, SA 5069. Tel/fax: 8-331-3057

Aspects, PO Box 2968, Rivonia 2128, SA (South Africa)
Tel: 11-864-1436

Realta, The Journal of the Irish Astrological Association, 4 Quay Street, Galway, Ireland. Available from IAA, 193, Lwr Rathmines Rd, Dublin 6, Ireland.

Astrological Association, 396 Caledonian Road, London, N1 1DN. Tel: (UK code) 0171 700 3746; Fax: 0171 700 6479. Bi-monthly journal issued.